Building MATH FLUENCY

Grades 4-6+

Consultant: Eleanor Falk Young
Editorial Development: Marilyn Evans
Copy Editing: Carrie Gwynne
Art Direction: Cheryl Puckett
Cover Design: Liliana Potigian
Illustration: Jo Larsen
Design/Production: Marcia Smith

EMC 3036

Evan-Moor®
EDUCATIONAL PUBLISHERS
Helping Children Learn since 1979

Visit
teaching-standards.com
to view a correlation
of this book.
This is a free service.

*Correlated to State and
Common Core State Standards*

Congratulations on your purchase of some of the finest teaching materials in the world.

Photocopying the pages in this book is permitted for <u>single-classroom use only</u>. Making photocopies for additional classes or schools is prohibited.

Contents

Building Math Fluency • EMC 3036 • © Evan-Moor Corp.

Test Your Skills

What's in This Book?

This book is intended for upper elementary students who need to master number facts. The goal of *Building Math Fluency* is to provide students with tools for thinking about computation in logical, strategic ways. Mastery of math facts is gained through understanding number patterns and number relationships.

Personalize Learning

Build Your Fact Power! on page 5 and *Learn Math Your Way* on page 6 help students take charge of their fact acquisition. In these pages and throughout the book, students are prompted to be active architects of their own learning. The learning aids on page 7 can be reproduced and laminated for individuals as needed.

Strategy Practice

Detailed strategy practice is provided for each number operation. These practice pages can be done with students in groups or individually. Students benefit from frequent modeling of computation strategies and sharing of solution steps.

Charts of the strategies are presented as reproducibles.

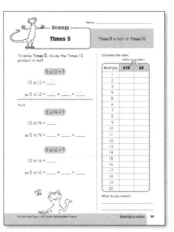

Practice pages feature a strategy box and problems to solve using that strategy.

Skill Building

The *Mixed Strategies Practice* and *Fact Power Skill Builders* pages provide opportunities to solidify and extend the learning of math fact strategies.

Test Your Skills

The *Test Your Skills* pages provide concentrated fact practice. These pages can be used in a number of ways, as described on page 105. A feature of *Test Your Skills* is the opportunity for students to evaluate their own progress.

Facts Flashcards

Reproducible flashcards for the operations covered in this book are provided. The teacher resource page at the beginning of the section gives suggestions for using the cards to enhance students' mastery of number facts.

Build Your Fact Power!

Train Like an Athlete

Why are math facts important?

Math facts help with all kinds of tasks. Think of the math needed to calculate sports scores, build a kite, make scenery for a play, plan a trip, budget, or cook a feast. For all of these activities, it helps to be able to compute accurately and easily. We call this ability **fact power**.

How do I improve my fact power?

Train like an athlete to develop your fact power. Conduct regular sessions to learn math facts so well that they come automatically. Here's how:

Set Goals
- Start with specific goals.
- Learn a few math facts very well.
- Build on these.

Practice Daily
- Train every day. Olympians do.
- Set aside time to work on math facts.
- Work out for twenty minutes each day.

Focus Intensely
- Concentrate <u>only</u> on math facts.
- Think about helpful strategies.
- Try new methods to compute.

Establish Routines
- Include regular warm-ups: skip count orally, practice with flashcards, write down key facts.

Make It Personal
- Think about how you learn best.
- Use *Learn Math Your Way* ideas on page 6 to build on your strengths.

Share
- Tell people about your goals.
- Enlist their help. Find out the strategies they use to compute.

Recap Nightly
- At bedtime, review the facts you've learned. See them in your mind, say them out loud, or trace them in the air.

Celebrate!
- Keep track of your learning.
- Each accomplishment matters.
- It all adds up.

Name _____

Learn Math Your Way

People learn in different ways. Some people need to draw pictures or diagrams. Some people learn best when they say things out loud. Others need to build with their hands and move their bodies to remember information.

How do *you* learn? What helps you to understand new ideas?

- Do you like to see ideas written down?
- Do pictures and diagrams make information clearer to you?
- Do discussions bring ideas alive in your mind?
- Is it best when you use counters to demonstrate an idea?
- Do you like to move around as you learn?

Personalize learning to your style. Here are some ideas for learning math your way:

Think in Pictures

- Make posters that include diagrams to explain math strategies.
- Draw pictures that represent key math facts.
- Color-code important flashcards.
- Use or visualize a number line or a number chart.

Think in Words

- Read the math strategies summaries out loud.
- Explain math strategies to an adult at home.
- Make up a song or a rhyme to remember math facts.
- Say what you are doing as you do it.

Think in Actions

- Move a finger or an object on a number line to compute.
- Trace flashcard problems with a highlighter.
- Write and solve math facts in the air.
- Clap while skip counting (3, 6, 9, 12 …).
- Bounce a ball or pace while practicing math facts.

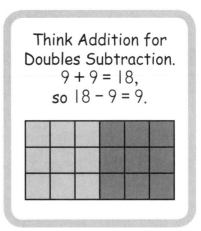

Think Addition for Doubles Subtraction.
9 + 9 = 18,
so 18 − 9 = 9.

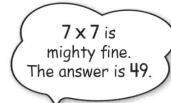

7 x 7 is mighty fine. The answer is 49.

Computation Tools

Number Lines

25	51	77
24	50	76
23	49	75
22	48	74
21	47	73
20	46	72
19	45	71
18	44	70
17	43	69
16	42	68
15	41	67
14	40	66
13	39	65
12	38	64
11	37	63
10	36	62
9	35	61
8	34	60
7	33	59
6	32	58
5	31	57
4	30	56
3	29	55
2	28	54
1	27	53
0	26	52

Number Chart

1	2	3	4	5	6	7	8	9	10
11	12	13	14	15	16	17	18	19	20
21	22	23	24	25	26	27	28	29	30
31	32	33	34	35	36	37	38	39	40
41	42	43	44	45	46	47	48	49	50
51	52	53	54	55	56	57	58	59	60
61	62	63	64	65	66	67	68	69	70
71	72	73	74	75	76	77	78	79	80
81	82	83	84	85	86	87	88	89	90
91	92	93	94	95	96	97	98	99	100
101	102	103	104	105	106	107	108	109	110
111	112	113	114	115	116	117	118	119	120
121	122	123	124	125	126	127	128	129	130
131	132	133	134	135	136	137	138	139	140
141	142	143	144	145	146	147	148	149	150
151	152	153	154	155	156	157	158	159	160
161	162	163	164	165	166	167	168	169	170
171	172	173	174	175	176	177	178	179	180
181	182	183	184	185	186	187	188	189	190
191	192	193	194	195	196	197	198	199	200

Glossary of Mathematics Terms

Addends The numbers in an addition problem.

$$3 + 4 = 7$$

addend   sum

Commutative Property of Addition Numbers can be added in any order without changing the sum.

$$3 + 4 = 7 \qquad 4 + 3 = 7$$

Commutative Property of Multiplication Factors can be multiplied in any order without changing the product.

$$3 \times 4 = 12 \qquad 4 \times 3 = 12$$

Difference The result of subtracting two numbers.

$$16 - 7 = 9$$

difference

Digit Any of the symbols 0, 1, 2, 3, 4, 5, 6, 7, 8, 9 used to write a number.

Fact Family A group of related facts, either addition and subtraction, or multiplication and division.

$$8 + 4 = 12 \qquad 4 + 8 = 12 \qquad 12 - 4 = 8 \qquad 12 - 8 = 4$$

Factors The numbers being multiplied.

$$3 \times 4 = 12$$

factor

Identity Property of Addition When 0 is added to a number, it does not change the total.

Identity Property of Multiplication The product of 1 and any number is that number.

$$1 \times 9 = 9 \qquad 49 \times 1 = 49$$

Minuend The number being subtracted from.

$$16 - 7 = 9$$

minuend

Multiples The product of a number and any whole number. For example, multiples of 4 are 0, 4, 8, 12, 16, etc.

Place Value The value of a digit as determined by its position in the ones place, tens place, etc. Each position is ten times of the place to its right and one-tenth of the place to its left.

Product The result of multiplication.

$$3 \times 4 = 12$$

product

Quotient The result of division.

$$12 \div 4 = 3$$

quotient

Subtrahend The number being subtracted.

$$16 - 7 = 9$$

subtrahend

Sum The result of joining quantities; the total.

$$3 + 4 = 7$$

sum

Building Math Fluency • EMC 3036 • © Evan-Moor Corp.

Teaching Addition Strategies

Pages 11–31 present practice with addition strategies that promote fact mastery and build computational fluency through focus on important number relationships and patterns.

Count Up   An efficient strategy to use when adding a small quantity to a larger quantity. Students start with the larger addend and count up the smaller addend to find the sum.

Tens Partners   Tens Partners are number pairs that make 10:

$$0 + 10, \ 1 + 9, \ 2 + 8, \ 3 + 7, \ 4 + 6, \ 5 + 5$$

Students can use Tens Partners when they are finding sums of 20.
For example: $12 + 8 = 10 + (2 + 8) = 10 + 10$

Doubles   Facts in which an addend is added to itself (example: $4 + 4$). Students discover that Doubles have even sums. When students have learned the Doubles facts, they have an "anchor" from which to compute many other facts.

Doubles Plus 1 means double the addend and add one more.
Doubles Plus 2 means double the addend and add two more.

Doubles Fact	Doubles Plus 1	Doubles Plus 2
$6 + 6 = 12$	$6 + 7 = 13$	$6 + 8 = 14$

Plus 10   When 10 is added to a number, the tens-place digit increases by one, while the ones-place digit remains the same (example: $44 + 10 = \underline{5}4$).

Note: When adding 10 to a number that has a 9 in the tens place, you make 10 tens, or 100 (example: $94 + 10 = \underline{10}4$).

Plus 9   This strategy is based on the fact that 9 is one away from 10.

Plus 8   This strategy is based on the fact that 8 is two away from 10.

See 9. Think 10.	See 8. Think 10.
See $6 + 9$. Think $6 + 10 - 1$.	See $6 + 8$. Think $6 + 10 - 2$.

Add in Small Steps   This strategy is based on the fact that it's easy to add a number to 10 or to a multiple of 10. Split the smaller addend into two parts, with one of those parts being the amount needed to make 10. For example:

$$35 + 7 = 35 + 5 + 2 = 40 + 2 = 42$$

Hidden Facts   Find Tens Partners or Doubles hidden within problems to make computing easier.

	Hidden Tens Partners	Hidden Doubles
$7 + 5 = ?$	$7 + 3 + 2$	$6 + 6$
$6 + 8 = ?$	$6 + 4 + 4$ $8 + 2 + 4$	$6 + 6 + 2$ $7 + 7$

Addition Strategies

Count Up	Count up from the larger number. Use when adding on 1, 2, 3, or 4.
Tens Partners	There are six sets of number pairs that make 10: $\quad$ 10 + 0 $\quad\quad$ 9 + 1 $\quad\quad$ 8 + 2 $\quad\quad$ 7 + 3 $\quad\quad$ 6 + 4 $\quad\quad$ 5 + 5 .... Tens Partners can be extended to the sums of 20. Make the ones-place digits Tens Partners. $\quad\quad$ 12 + 8, 16 + 4
Doubles	Add the number to itself and that number doubles. $\quad\quad$ 2 + 2 = 4 $\quad\quad$ 6 + 6 = 12
Doubles Plus 1	Double the number and add one more. If you know 7 + 7 = 14, then 7 + 8 is one more, or 15.
Doubles Plus 2	Double the number and add two more. If you know 5 + 5 = 10, then 5 + 7 is two more, or 12.
Plus 10	When 10 is added to a number, the tens-place digit increases by one. $\quad\quad$ 23 + 10 = 33
Plus 9 **See 9. Think 10.**	Add 10 and subtract 1. $\quad\quad$ Example: 18 + 9 $\quad\quad$ Think: 18 + 10 = 28 $\quad$ so $\quad$ 18 + 9 is one less, or 27. .... Plus 9 can be extended to Plus 19: Add 20 and subtract 1. Plus 9 can be extended to Plus 99: Add 100 and subtract 1.
Plus 8 **See 8. Think 10.**	Add 10 and subtract 2.
Add in Small Steps	Split the smaller number into two parts so that you can add up to a multiple of 10. For example: 26 + 7 = ? 1. The Tens Partner for **6** in **26** is 4. So, split 7 into 4 + 3. 2. Add the Tens Partners numbers: 26 + 4 = 30 3. Then add the remaining number: 30 + 3 = 33
Hidden Facts	Finding Tens Partners and Doubles hidden within problems can make the problems easier to solve. 	Hidden Tens Partners	Hidden Doubles	 |---|---| 	8 + 6 = (8 + 2) + 4	6 + 8 = (6 + 6) + 2	 	$\quad\quad$ = 10 + 4	$\quad\quad$ = 12 + 2	 	$\quad\quad$ = 14	$\quad\quad$ = 14	

Strategy

Count Up

Count Up from the largest addend.
Use when adding on 1, 2, 3, or 4.

Count on the larger number.

9, 10, 11

$8 + 3 =$ _11_

20, 21

$19 + 2 =$ _____

$28 + 4 =$ _____

$37 + 3 =$ _____

$79 + 2 =$ _____

$67 + 4 =$ _____

$199 + 2 =$ _____

$228 + 4 =$ _____

$1,109 + 1 =$ _____

Start with the larger number and count on the smaller number.

18, 19, 20, 21

$17 + 4 =$ _21_

$2 + 18 =$ _____

$39 + 4 =$ _____

$3 + 397 =$ _____

$178 + 2 =$ _____

$66 + 4 =$ _____

$2 + 229 =$ _____

$4 + 997 =$ _____

$1,099 + 1 =$ _____

$1,007 + 4 =$ _____

$998 + 3 =$ _____

$1,529 + 3 =$ _____

$9,999 + 1 =$ _____

$3 + 1,097 =$ _____

$2 + 9,999 =$ _____

How do you solve Count Up problems? (Check all that apply.)

❑ Count to myself   ❑ Tap pencil

❑ Imagine a number line   ❑ Other: _____

Tens Partners

Number pairs that make 10 are called **Tens Partners**.

The number pairs with sums of 10 are: 10+0, 9+1, 8+2, 7+3, 6+4, 5+5
Below are four ways to think about **Tens Partners**.
Which one makes the most sense to you?
Make a ★ by it.

1 **Ten-Frame Dots**

3 **Number Pattern**

$$0 + 10 = 10$$
$$1 + 9 = 10$$
$$2 + 8 = 10$$
$$3 + 7 = 10$$
$$4 + 6 = 10$$
$$5 + 5 = 10$$
$$6 + 4 = 10$$
$$7 + 3 = 10$$
$$8 + 2 = 10$$
$$9 + 1 = 10$$

2 **Tens Staircase**

1		9	
2		8	
3		7	
4		6	
5		5	
6		4	
7		3	
8		2	
9		1	
10			

4 **Finger Combinations**

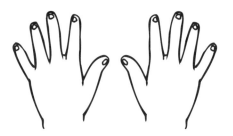

Example: 5 + 5

Strategy

Tens Partners

Tens Partners are the number pairs that make 10.

Tens Partners help solve many other addition and subtraction problems.
It is important to know the **Tens Partners** by heart.

Complete the **Tens Partners** equations.

$8 + 2 = $ _____ $6 + $ _____ $ = 10$ _____ $ + 3 = 10$

$1 + $ _____ $ = 10$ _____ $ + 2 = 10$ $5 + $ _____ $ = 10$

Solve the **Tens Partners** problems.
Leave the other problems blank.

$$\begin{array}{r} 6 \\ + 3 \\ \hline \end{array} \qquad \begin{array}{r} 9 \\ + 1 \\ \hline \end{array} \qquad \begin{array}{r} 2 \\ + 9 \\ \hline \end{array} \qquad \begin{array}{r} 5 \\ + 5 \\ \hline \end{array} \qquad \begin{array}{r} 2 \\ + 7 \\ \hline \end{array} \qquad \begin{array}{r} 2 \\ + 8 \\ \hline \end{array} \qquad \begin{array}{r} 6 \\ + 4 \\ \hline \end{array}$$

$$\begin{array}{r} 5 \\ + 6 \\ \hline \end{array} \qquad \begin{array}{r} 3 \\ + 7 \\ \hline \end{array} \qquad \begin{array}{r} 4 \\ + 6 \\ \hline \end{array} \qquad \begin{array}{r} 5 \\ + 4 \\ \hline \end{array} \qquad \begin{array}{r} 7 \\ + 4 \\ \hline \end{array} \qquad \begin{array}{r} 9 \\ + 0 \\ \hline \end{array} \qquad \begin{array}{r} 3 \\ + 8 \\ \hline \end{array}$$

What helps you to recognize **Tens Partners**?

_____

_____

_____

Strategy
Tens Partners Extended

Tens Partners can be used to make sums of 20 and other multiples of 10 (30, 40, 50, and so on).

Join the **Tens Partners** to make sums of 20.

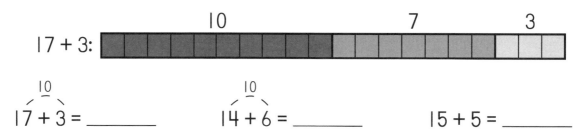

$17 + 3$:

$17 + 3 =$ _____ $14 + 6 =$ _____ $15 + 5 =$ _____

Complete the missing **Tens Partner** to make 20.

$16 +$ _____ $= 20$ $11 +$ _____ $= 20$ _____ $+ 12 = 20$

$18 +$ _____ $= 20$ $13 +$ _____ $= 20$ _____ $+ 14 = 20$

Think **Tens Partners** to make Hundreds Partners.

$90 +$ _____ $= 100$ $80 +$ _____ $= 100$ $70 +$ _____ $= 100$

$60 +$ _____ $= 100$ $50 +$ _____ $= 100$ $40 +$ _____ $= 100$

Try these.

$95 +$ _____ $= 100$ $85 +$ _____ $= 100$ $75 +$ _____ $= 100$

$65 +$ _____ $= 100$ $55 +$ _____ $= 100$ $45 +$ _____ $= 100$

$35 +$ _____ $= 100$ $25 +$ _____ $= 100$ $15 +$ _____ $= 100$

$94 +$ _____ $= 100$ $88 +$ _____ $= 100$ $73 +$ _____ $= 100$

Strategy

Hidden Tens Partners

Tens Partners can be hidden in problems.

Hidden Tens Partners is a fast way to add.

$$8 + 6 = \overset{\overset{10}{\frown}}{8 + 2} + 4$$

Count Up is slow → 8 + 6

Find **Hidden Tens Partners**.

	Tens Partners + _____	Sum
7 + 6	7 + 3 + 3	13
8 + 5		
9 + 6		
8 + 7		
Write your own.		

Hidden Tens Partners Steps

1 Start with the larger addend.

2 Determine what is needed to make 10.

3 Add on this amount. Then add the rest.

Strategy
Hidden Tens Partners

Tens Partners can be hidden in problems.

Look at the **Hidden Tens Partners** in these equations.

$$18 + 4 \rightarrow 1\overset{20}{8 + 2} + 2 = 22$$

15 16 17 (18) 19 20 21 22 23 24 25

$$35 + 8 \rightarrow 3\overset{40}{5 + 5} + 3 = 43$$

(35) 36 37 38 39 40 41 42 43 44 45

Find the hidden **Tens Partners**.
Show your work.

$$17 + 6 = \underline{1\overset{20}{7 + 3} + 3 = 20 + 3 = 23}$$

$16 + 8 =$ _____

$18 + 5 =$ _____

$26 + 5 =$ _____

$37 + 8 =$ _____

$45 + 7 =$ _____

$58 + 8 =$ _____

Building Math Fluency • EMC 3036 • © Evan-Moor Corp.

Strategy

Doubles

Add a number to itself.

Doubles facts can help you solve many addition, subtraction, multiplication, and division problems. Here are two ways to think about **Doubles** facts.

1 **Numeric Pattern**

1 + 1 = _____   6 + 6 = _____

2 + 2 = _____   7 + 7 = _____

3 + 3 = _____   8 + 8 = _____

4 + 4 = _____   9 + 9 = _____

5 + 5 = _____   10 + 10 = _____

What do you notice about the sums? _____

2 **Visual Pattern** building on Double 5

6 + 6 = _____

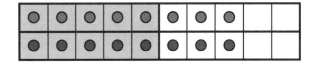

8 + 8 = _____

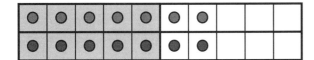

7 + 7 = _____

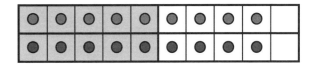

9 + 9 = _____

Doubles Extended

Name _____

Add a number to itself.

Solve the **Doubles** problems.

11 + 11 = _____   15 + 15 = _____   19 + 19 = _____

12 + 12 = _____   16 + 16 = _____   20 + 20 = _____

13 + 13 = _____   17 + 17 = _____   25 + 25 = _____

14 + 14 = _____   18 + 18 = _____   26 + 26 = _____

If $4 + 4 = 8$, then $40 + 40 = 80$.

If $4 + 4 = 8$, then $400 + 400 = 800$.

Solve bigger **Doubles** facts.

50 + 50 = _____   500 + 500 = _____

60 + 60 = _____   600 + 600 = _____

70 + 70 = _____   700 + 700 = _____

80 + 80 = _____   800 + 800 = _____

90 + 90 = _____   900 + 900 = _____

6,000 + 6,000 = _____   8,000 + 8,000 = _____

7,000 + 7,000 = _____   9,000 + 9,000 = _____

Strategy

Hidden Doubles

Look for **Doubles** hidden in problems.

When you know **Doubles**, you also know related facts.

Doubles: $5 + 5 = 10$ Double the number.

Doubles +1: $5 + 6 = 11$ Double the number and add one more.

Doubles +2: $5 + 7 = 12$ Double the number and add two more.

Find the **Hidden Doubles**.

	Doubles Fact + _____	Sum
5 + 6	5 + 5 + 1	11
7 + 8		
8 + 9		
15 + 16		
6 + 8	6 + 6 + 2	14
7 + 9		
15 + 17		
24 + 26		
Write your own.		

Name _____

Brain Stretchers

Solve the problems using **Tens Partners** and **Doubles** facts.

Tens Partners

$997 + 3 =$ _____

$997 + 13 =$ _____

$1,997 + 13 =$ _____

$5 + 5 =$ _____

$55 + 5 =$ _____

$55 + 55 =$ _____

$555 + 55 =$ _____

$8 + 2 =$ _____

$98 + 2 =$ _____

$98 + 12 =$ _____

$98 + 112 =$ _____

$98 +$ _____ $= 310$

Doubles Facts

$6 + 6 =$ _____

$56 + 6 =$ _____

$56 + 56 =$ _____

$7 + 7 =$ _____

$17 + 7 =$ _____

$17 + 17 =$ _____

$27 + 27 =$ _____

$8 + 8 =$ _____

$16 + 16 =$ _____

$32 + 32 =$ _____

$64 + 64 =$ _____

$128 + 128 =$ _____

Strategy

Plus 10 Extended

Add 10 to a number, and the tens-place digit increases by one. Add 20, and the tens-place digit increases by two, and so forth.

Plus 10
Add one 10.

17 + 10 = _____

38 + 10 = _____

49 + 10 = _____

72 + 10 = _____

95 + 10 = _____

_____ + 10 = _____

Plus 20
Add two 10s.

17 + 20 = _____

38 + 20 = _____

49 + 20 = _____

72 + 20 = _____

95 + 20 = _____

_____ + 20 = _____

Plus 100
Add one 100.

170 + 100 = _____

380 + 100 = _____

490 + 100 = _____

720 + 100 = _____

950 + 100 = _____

_____ + 100 = _____

Plus 200
Add two 100s.

170 + 200 = _____

380 + 200 = _____

490 + 200 = _____

720 + 200 = _____

950 + 200 = _____

_____ + 200 = _____

Strategy

Plus 9

See 9. Think 10.
For **Plus 9**, add 10 and subtract 1.

Turn **Plus 9** problems into **Plus 10** problems
because 9 is just one away from 10.

$$14 + 9 \rightarrow 1\overset{24}{\overbrace{4 + 1}}0 - 1 = 23$$

Solve.

16 + 9 = _____   25 + 9 = _____   19 + 9 = _____

33 + 9 = _____   14 + 9 = _____   27 + 9 = _____

48 + 9 = _____   18 + 9 = _____   43 + 9 = _____

Strategy

Plus 8

See 8. Think 10.
For **Plus 8**, add 10 and subtract 2.

Turn **Plus 8** problems into **Plus 10** problems
because 8 is just two away from 10.

$$14 + 8 \rightarrow 1\overset{24}{\overbrace{4 + 1}}0 - 2 = 22$$

Solve.

16 + 8 = _____   25 + 8 = _____   19 + 8 = _____

33 + 8 = _____   14 + 8 = _____   27 + 8 = _____

48 + 8 = _____   18 + 8 = _____   43 + 8 = _____

Building Math Fluency • EMC 3036 • © Evan-Moor Corp.

Strategy

Plus 19

See 19. Think 20.
For **Plus 19**, add 20 and subtract 1.

Turn **Plus 19** problems into **Plus 20** problems
because 19 is just one away from 20.

$$14 + 19 \rightarrow 1\overset{34}{\overbrace{4 + 20}} - 1 = 33$$

Solve.

25 + 19 = _____   33 + 19 = _____   48 + 19 = _____

57 + 19 = _____   66 + 19 = _____   75 + 19 = _____

Strategy

Plus 99

See 99. Think 100.
For **Plus 99**, add 100
and subtract 1.

Turn **Plus 99** problems into **Plus 100** problems
because 99 is just one away from 100.

$$140 + 99 \rightarrow 1\overset{240}{\overbrace{40 + 100}} - 1 = 239$$

Solve.

150 + 99 = _____   260 + 99 = _____   180 + 99 = _____

331 + 99 = _____   142 + 99 = _____   273 + 99 = _____

Write and solve a **Plus 99** problem of your own.

_____

Mixed Strategies Practice

Name _____

Brain Benders

Warm-up

17	28	45	86	34
+ 10	+ 9	+ 10	+ 9	+ 9

Complete each equation.
Is it **9** or **10**?

18 + _____ = 28   25 + _____ = 34   19 + _____ = 29

37 + _____ = 46   88 + _____ = 98   27 + _____ = 36

Write the missing addend.
Is it **19** or **20**?

22	48	31	31	65
+ ___	+ ___	+ ___	+ ___	+ ___
42	67	50	51	84

Write the missing addend.
Is it **99** or **100**?

47	81	85	110	110
+ ___	+ ___	+ ___	+ ___	+ ___
147	180	184	210	209

   Building Math Fluency • EMC 3036 • © Evan-Moor Corp.

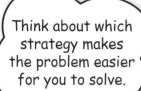

Name _____

Many Ways to Add

$$8 + 6 = ?$$

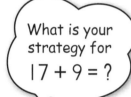

Think about which strategy makes the problem easier for you to solve.

I see **Tens Partners**.

$$8 + 6 = 8 + 2 + 4$$
$$= 10 + 4$$
$$= 14$$

I see **Doubles**.

$$6 + 8 = 6 + 6 + 2$$
$$= 12 + 2$$
$$= 14$$

Think about the problems. Choose a strategy. Show your work.

What is your strategy for
$$17 + 9 = ?$$

My strategy was _____.

What is your strategy for
$$28 + 8 = ?$$

My strategy was _____.

Name _____

Name That Strategy

===== Strategy Names =====

Doubles   Doubles + 1   Plus 9   Plus 19   ~~Tens Partners~~   Hundreds Partners

Solve the problems.
Write the strategy name.

Strategy name
Tens Partners

4 + 6 = _____

8 + 2 = _____

1 + 9 = _____

7 + 3 = _____

5 + 5 = _____

2 + 8 = _____

Strategy name

90 + 10 = _____

70 + 30 = _____

60 + 40 = _____

20 + 80 = _____

25 + 75 = _____

15 + 85 = _____

Strategy name

6 + 9 = _____

8 + 9 = _____

12 + 9 = _____

15 + 9 = _____

26 + 9 = _____

34 + 9 = _____

Strategy name

26 + 19 = _____

38 + 19 = _____

42 + 19 = _____

55 + 19 = _____

66 + 19 = _____

74 + 19 = _____

Strategy name

6 + 6 = _____

8 + 8 = _____

9 + 9 = _____

7 + 7 = _____

12 + 12 = _____

15 + 15 = _____

Strategy name

6 + 7 = _____

8 + 9 = _____

9 + 10 = _____

7 + 8 = _____

12 + 13 = _____

15 + 16 = _____

Building Math Fluency • EMC 3036 • © Evan-Moor Corp.

Name _____

Skill Builders +4, +5, +6

Think about addition strategies. Solve.

+4	+5	+6
5 + 4 = _____	6 + 5 = _____	5 + 6 = _____
6 + 4 = _____	8 + 5 = _____	6 + 6 = _____
9 + 4 = _____	9 + 5 = _____	9 + 6 = _____
7 + 4 = _____	7 + 5 = _____	7 + 6 = _____
8 + 4 = _____	2 + 5 = _____	8 + 6 = _____
3 + 4 = _____	12 + 5 = _____	3 + 6 = _____
11 + 4 = _____	15 + 5 = _____	11 + 6 = _____
12 + 4 = _____	11 + 5 = _____	12 + 6 = _____
15 + 4 = _____	10 + 5 = _____	10 + 6 = _____
18 + 4 = _____	14 + 5 = _____	18 + 6 = _____
16 + 4 = _____	16 + 5 = _____	16 + 6 = _____
14 + 4 = _____	18 + 5 = _____	14 + 6 = _____
10 + 4 = _____	13 + 5 = _____	17 + 6 = _____

Fact Power
Skill Builders

Name _____

Skill Builders +7, +8, +9

Use addition strategies to solve.

+7	+8	+9
5 + 7 = _____	6 + 8 = _____	5 + 9 = _____
6 + 7 = _____	8 + 8 = _____	6 + 9 = _____
9 + 7 = _____	9 + 8 = _____	9 + 9 = _____
7 + 7 = _____	7 + 8 = _____	7 + 9 = _____
8 + 7 = _____	2 + 8 = _____	8 + 9 = _____
3 + 7 = _____	4 + 8 = _____	3 + 9 = _____
11 + 7 = _____	15 + 8 = _____	11 + 9 = _____
12 + 7 = _____	11 + 8 = _____	12 + 9 = _____
13 + 7 = _____	16 + 8 = _____	15 + 9 = _____
10 + 7 = _____	14 + 8 = _____	13 + 9 = _____
16 + 7 = _____	10 + 8 = _____	16 + 9 = _____
14 + 7 = _____	12 + 8 = _____	14 + 9 = _____
17 + 7 = _____	13 + 8 = _____	10 + 9 = _____

Building Math Fluency • EMC 3036 • © Evan-Moor Corp.

Name _____

Skip Count by 10

Skip Count up by 10s to practice adding 10 to a number.

Skip Count back by 10s to practice subtracting 10 from a number.

Use the number chart.

1	2	3	4	5	6	7	8	9	10
11	12	13	14	15	16	17	18	19	20
21	22	23	24	25	26	27	28	29	30
31	32	33	34	35	36	37	38	39	40
41	42	43	44	45	46	47	48	49	50
51	52	53	54	55	56	57	58	59	60

Start at **4**. Skip Count **up** by 10s.

4, 14, ____, ____, ____, ____, ____, ____, ____, ____, ____, ____, ____, 134

Start at **154**. Skip Count **back** by 10s.

154, ____, ____, ____, ____, ____, ____, ____, ____, ____, ____, 34

Start at **6**. Skip Count **up** by 10s.

6, 16, ____, ____, ____, ____, ____, ____, ____, ____, ____, ____, ____, 136

Start at **176**. Skip Count **back** by 10s.

176, ____, ____, ____, ____, ____, ____, ____, ____, ____, ____, 56

Start at **17**. Skip Count **up** by 10s.

17, 27, ____, ____, ____, ____, ____, ____, ____, ____, ____, ____, ____, 147

Start at **147**. Skip Count **back** by 10s.

147, ____, ____, ____, ____, ____, ____, ____, ____, ____, ____, 17

Name _____

Skip Count by 10, 20, 25

Skip Count up and back. Clap, tap, or nod as you count.

Start at **3**. Skip Count **up** by 10s.

3, 13, ____, ____, ____, ____, ____, ____, ____, ____, ____, ____, ____

Start at **113**. Skip Count **back** by 10s.

113, ____, ____, ____, ____, ____, ____, ____, ____, ____, ____, ____

Start at **0**. Skip Count **up** by 20s.

0, 20, ____, ____, ____, ____, ____, ____, ____, ____, ____, ____, 260

Start at **260**. Skip Count **back** by 20s.

260, ____, ____, ____, ____, ____, ____, ____, ____, ____, ____, ____, 0

Start at **0**. Skip Count **up** by 25s.

0, 25, ____, ____, ____, ____, ____, ____, ____, ____, ____, ____, 325

Start at **325**. Skip Count **back** by 25s.

325, ____, ____, ____, ____, ____, ____, ____, ____, ____, ____, ____, 0

Start at [ ]. Skip Count **back** by [ ].

____, ____, ____, ____, ____, ____, ____, ____, ____, ____, ____, ____

Building Math Fluency • EMC 3036 • © Evan-Moor Corp.

Name _____

Addition by Design

Use addition strategies to solve each problem.
Color as directed in the chart below.

2 + 98	15 + 4	6 + 7	17 + 3	4 + 11	8 + 9	30 + 70
4 + 9	6 + 4	14 + 6	50 + 50	7 + 3	13 + 7	6 + 11
10 + 7	5 + 5	91 + 9	75 + 25	20 + 80	10 + 10	7 + 4
1 + 9	3 + 97	8 + 92	11 + 9	40 + 60	1 + 99	8 + 12
9 + 6	4 + 16	10 + 90	45 + 55	96 + 4	15 + 5	4 + 21
13 + 4	18 + 2	3 + 7	95 + 5	19 + 1	10 + 0	10 + 5
93 + 7	13 + 6	4 + 5	2 + 8	10 + 9	2 + 3	94 + 6

Sum	Color
10 or 20	yellow
100	red
Odd number	blue

Teaching Subtraction Strategies

Pages 34–50 present practice with subtraction strategies that promote computational fluency and fact mastery.

There are two ways to look at subtraction:

- as the reduction of an amount
  "If I take 7 away from 16, I have 9 left."

- as the comparison of two quantities
  "The difference between 16 and 7 is 9."

$$\overset{\text{minuend}}{\downarrow}16 - \underset{\underset{\text{subtrahend}}{\uparrow}}{7} = 9 \leftarrow \text{difference}$$

Count Back	Also thought of as *take away.* This strategy is best when subtracting a small number (1, 2, or 3) from a larger number.
	For 19 − 2, start at 19 and count back 2 to get to 17.
Count Up	Count up from the lower number to find the difference between the two quantities. This strategy is best when the minuend and subtrahend are close together.
	For 99 − 97, count up 2 from 97 to 99.
Think Addition	Turn subtraction into addition problems. Students usually master addition facts first. This strategy allows them to use facts they know to compute new facts.
	Turn 17 − 12 = ☐ into ☐ + 12 = 17. Think: *What* + 12 is 17?
Tens Partners	If you know the sums of 10 (Tens Partners), then you know the related subtraction facts:
	10 − 9 = 1 10 − 8 = 2 10 − 7 = 3
Doubles	If you know addition Doubles, then you know the related subtraction facts:
	18 − 9 = 9 16 − 8 = 8 14 − 7 = 7
Minus 10 Minus 9 Minus 8	Just as students learn patterns with Plus 10, they apply the opposite patterns to Minus 10. This can be extended to Minus 9 and Minus 8:
	See 9. Think 10. See 16 − 9. Think 16 − 10 and add 1.
	See 8. Think 10. See 15 − 8. Think 15 − 10 and add 2.
Subtract in Small Steps	This strategy is based on the fact that it's easy to subtract from 10 or a multiple of 10. Split the subtrahend into two parts, with one of those parts being the amount you need to subtract to get to a multiple of 10. For example:
	For 15 − 6 try 15 − 5 − 1
	For 24 − 7 try 24 − 4 − 3

Subtraction Strategies

Count Back	Count back to take away small numbers, such as 1, 2, or 3.
Count Up	Count up to find the difference. This works best when the numbers are close together. $11 - 9 = \square$ Count up from 9 to 11.
Think Addition	To subtract, think of the related addition fact. $13 - 6 = \square$ Think: $\square + 6 = 13$
Tens Partners	If you know the addition Tens Partners, then you know the related subtraction facts. $7 + 3 = 10$ so $10 - 3 = 7$ and $10 - 7 = 3$ . . . . Tens Partners can be extended to find differences from 20. $20 - 8 = 12$
Doubles	If you know the addition Doubles facts, then you know the related subtraction facts. $2 + 2 = 4$ so $4 - 2 = 2$
Minus 10	The tens-place digit decreases by one, and the ones-place digit stays the same. $23 - 10 = 13$
Minus 9 See 9. Think 10.	Subtract 10 and add 1. . . . . Minus 9 can be extended to Minus 19: Subtract 20 and add 1. Minus 9 can be extended to Minus 99: Subtract 100 and add 1.
Minus 8 See 8. Think 10.	Subtract 10 and add 2.
Subtract in Small Steps	Split the number being subtracted into two parts so that you can subtract to 10 or a multiple of 10. For example: $24 - 7 = \square$ $24 - 4 = 20$. So, split 7 into 4 and 3. Then apply Tens Partners to subtract 3 from 20. $20 - 3 = 17$

Strategy

Count Back

Count Back to take away small numbers, such as 1, 2, or 3.

There are many ways to **Count Back**.

See It.

Picture a number line in your mind.

$$11 - 3 = 8$$

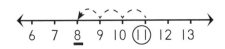

6 7 _8_ 9 10 ⑪ 12 13

Say It.

Count back in your mind.

10, 9, 8

$$11 - 3 = 8$$

Move It.

Tap your pencil or make dots.

● ● ●

$$11 - 3 = 8$$

Count Back is a quick way to subtract small numbers.

$16 - 2 =$ _____ $13 - 2 =$ _____ $18 - 3 =$ _____

$18 - 1 =$ _____ $17 - 2 =$ _____ $12 - 3 =$ _____

$19 - 2 =$ _____ $15 - 2 =$ _____ $14 - 3 =$ _____

Count Back to subtract.

$79 - 2 =$ _____ $51 - 2 =$ _____ $88 - 3 =$ _____

$1,000 - 1 =$ _____ $21 - 3 =$ _____ $42 - 3 =$ _____

$101 - 2 =$ _____ $31 - 2 =$ _____ $33 - 3 =$ _____

$55 - \boxed{} = 53$ $61 - \boxed{} = 59$ $12 - \boxed{} = 9$

Strategy

Count Up

Count Up to find the difference. This works best when the numbers are close together.

Count Up to find the difference when the numbers are close together.

Think about: 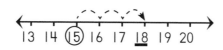 $18 - 15 = ?$ Counting up 3 is quick.

13 14 ⑮ 16 17 18 19 20

Find the difference.
Count Up from the bottom number.

$$\begin{array}{r} 22 \\ -\ 18 \\ \hline \end{array} \qquad \begin{array}{r} 15 \\ -\ 13 \\ \hline \end{array} \qquad \begin{array}{r} 20 \\ -\ 17 \\ \hline \end{array} \qquad \begin{array}{r} 12 \\ -\ 9 \\ \hline \end{array} \qquad \begin{array}{r} 18 \\ -\ 13 \\ \hline \end{array}$$

$$\begin{array}{r} 13 \\ -\ 9 \\ \hline \end{array} \qquad \begin{array}{r} 21 \\ -\ 19 \\ \hline \end{array} \qquad \begin{array}{r} 19 \\ -\ 16 \\ \hline \end{array} \qquad \begin{array}{r} 11 \\ -\ 8 \\ \hline \end{array} \qquad \begin{array}{r} 14 \\ -\ 9 \\ \hline \end{array}$$

Count Back Review

Count Back is effective for taking away small amounts.

Think about: $18 - 3 = ?$ Counting back 3 is quick.

13 14 15 16 17 ⑱ 19 20

Count Back to subtract.

$$\begin{array}{r} 35 \\ -\ 3 \\ \hline \end{array} \qquad \begin{array}{r} 27 \\ -\ 2 \\ \hline \end{array} \qquad \begin{array}{r} 18 \\ -\ 2 \\ \hline \end{array} \qquad \begin{array}{r} 12 \\ -\ 1 \\ \hline \end{array} \qquad \begin{array}{r} 41 \\ -\ 3 \\ \hline \end{array}$$

Name _____

Which Way?

I'm confused. The subtraction sign means *take away*. I count back to take away. Right?

Subtraction also means to find the difference. You can **Count Back** or **Count Up**. Look at the numbers involved to decide which is quicker.

Count Back

Works best when subtracting small amounts like 1, 2, 3, or 4

Count Up

Works best when the numbers in the problem are close together

Circle the **Count Up** problems.
Solve all the problems.

25 − 1 = _____   71 − 1 = _____   21 − 2 = _____

60 − 58 = _____   97 − 95 = _____   31 − 29 = _____

19 − 2 = _____   29 − 28 = _____   20 − 3 = _____

53 − 49 = _____   78 − 4 = _____   63 − 2 = _____

91 − 88 = _____   42 − 39 = _____   87 − 3 = _____

Building Math Fluency • EMC 3036 • © Evan-Moor Corp.

Strategy

Tens Partners

Use **Tens Partners** addition to solve subtraction facts.

Think addition for **Tens Partners** subtraction.

$1 + 9 = 10$ so $10 - 1 = 9$ $7 + 3 = 10$ so $10 - 7 = 3$

Think **Tens Partners** addition to solve subtraction problems.

$10 - 1 =$ _____ $10 - 3 =$ _____ $10 - 6 =$ _____

$10 - 4 =$ _____ $10 - 8 =$ _____ $10 - 2 =$ _____

Apply **Tens Partners** to solve the problems.

$20 - 15 =$ _____ $20 - 13 =$ _____ $20 - 16 =$ _____

$20 - 18 =$ _____ $20 - 9 =$ _____ $20 - 12 =$ _____

$100 - 70 =$ _____ $100 - 75 =$ _____ $100 - 55 =$ _____

Complete the missing **Tens Partners**.

$$\begin{array}{r} 10 \\ - \\ \hline 6 \end{array} \qquad \begin{array}{r} 10 \\ - \\ \hline 2 \end{array} \qquad \begin{array}{r} 4 \\ + \\ \hline 10 \end{array} \qquad \begin{array}{r} 7 \\ + \\ \hline 10 \end{array} \qquad \begin{array}{r} 10 \\ - \\ \hline 1 \end{array}$$

Strategy

Doubles

Use **Doubles** addition to solve subtraction.

Imagine a candy bar. If you eat half, how many pieces will be left?

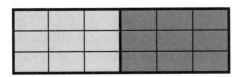

Solve this with **Doubles:** $9 + 9 = 18$, so $18 - 9 = 9$.

Do this **Doubles** warm-up.

Solve   **Match**

$8 + 8 =$ _____

$6 + 6 =$ _____

$7 + 7 =$ _____

$9 + 9 =$ _____

Think **Doubles** facts to subtract.

$20 - 10 =$ _____ $16 - 8 =$ _____ $12 - 6 =$ _____

$14 - 7 =$ _____ $18 - 9 =$ _____ $10 - 5 =$ _____

$$\begin{array}{r} 16 \\ -8 \\ \hline \end{array}$$
$$\begin{array}{r} 14 \\ -7 \\ \hline \end{array}$$
$$\begin{array}{r} 12 \\ -6 \\ \hline \end{array}$$
$$\begin{array}{r} 18 \\ -9 \\ \hline \end{array}$$

Strategy

Think Addition

To subtract, think of the related addition fact.

See **Subtraction**. Think **Addition**.

$$14 - 8 = \boxed{} \rightarrow \boxed{} + 8 = 14$$

I see $14 - 8$ and say to myself, "What plus 8 is 14?"

Think of the related addition fact to solve subtraction.

$\square + 12 = 19$

$19 - 12 =$ _____

$\square + 13 = 20$

$20 - 13 =$ _____

$\square + 9 = 13$

$13 - 9 =$ _____

$\square + 7 = 11$

$11 - 7 =$ _____

$\square + 9 = 14$

$14 - 9 =$ _____

$\square + 7 = 12$

$12 - 7 =$ _____

$15 - 11 =$ _____

$16 - 8 =$ _____

$13 - 6 =$ _____

$$\begin{array}{r} 15 \\ -\ 9 \\ \hline \end{array}$$

$$\begin{array}{r} 16 \\ -\ 11 \\ \hline \end{array}$$

$$\begin{array}{r} 19 \\ -\ 12 \\ \hline \end{array}$$

$$\begin{array}{r} 14 \\ -\ 8 \\ \hline \end{array}$$

Mixed Strategies Practice

Brain Boosters

Subtraction problems can be thought of as addition problems.
Match the facts and solve them.

16 − 14 = _____   •   _____ + 8 = 17

17 − 8 = _____   •   _____ + 14 = 16

14 − 7 = _____   •   _____ + 9 = 15

15 − 9 = _____   •   _____ + 7 = 14

Solve **Doubles** subtraction.

18 − 9 = _____   14 − 7 = _____   16 − 8 = _____

20 − 10 = _____   60 − 30 = _____   50 − 25 = _____

90 − 45 = _____   70 − 35 = _____   30 − 15 = _____

Determine the missing numbers for the **Doubles** subtraction equations.

84 − _____ = _____   62 − _____ = _____   36 − _____ = _____
    ↑   ↑   ↑   ↑   ↑   ↑
same number   same number   same number

48 − _____ = _____   24 − _____ = _____   70 − _____ = _____
    ↑   ↑   ↑   ↑   ↑   ↑
same number   same number   same number

Strategy

Minus 10
Minus 20

Subtract 10, and the tens-place digit decreases by one. Subtract 20, and the tens-place digit decreases by two.

Visualize a number chart.
Go back 10 for **Minus 10**.
Go back 20 for **Minus 20**.

Examples:
$$52 - 10 = 42$$
$$66 - 20 = 46$$

31	32	33	34	35	36	37	38	39	40
41	42	43	44	45	46	47	48	49	50
51	52	53	54	55	56	57	58	59	60
61	62	63	64	65	66	67	68	69	70
71	72	73	74	75	76	77	78	79	80

Subtract **10**.

$$17 - 10 = \underline{} \qquad 19 - 10 = \underline{} \qquad 12 - 10 = \underline{}$$

$$78 - 10 = \underline{} \qquad 43 - 10 = \underline{} \qquad 106 - 10 = \underline{}$$

Subtract **20**.

$$55 - 20 = \underline{} \qquad 86 - 20 = \underline{} \qquad 106 - 20 = \underline{}$$

Subtract **100**.

$$378 - 100 = \underline{} \qquad 143 - 100 = \underline{} \qquad 1{,}006 - 100 = \underline{}$$

Subtract **200**.

$$355 - 200 = \underline{} \qquad 486 - 200 = \underline{} \qquad 1{,}006 - 200 = \underline{}$$

$$\underline{} - 200 = 742 \qquad \underline{} - 200 = 360 \qquad \underline{} - 200 = 975$$

Name _____

Minus 9

For **Minus 9**,
subtract 10 and add 1.

Turn **Minus 9** problems into **Minus 10** problems
because 9 is just one away from 10.

For 14 − 9, think 14 − 10 and add 1.

Imagine a number line:

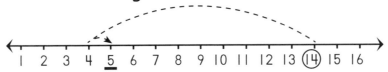

Go back 10
and up 1.

Write the equation like this:

$$14 - 9 = 14 - 10 + 1 = 5$$

Solve.

16 − 9 = _____   25 − 9 = _____   31 − 9 = _____

33 − 9 = _____   44 − 9 = _____   27 − 9 = _____

48 − 9 = _____   18 − 9 = _____   42 − 9 = _____

Subtract.

Minus 10	**Minus 9**	**Minus 8**
27 − 10 = _____	27 − 9 = _____	27 − 8 = _____
81 − 10 = _____	81 − 9 = _____	81 − 8 = _____
45 − 10 = _____	45 − 9 = _____	45 − 8 = _____

    Building Math Fluency • EMC 3036 • © Evan-Moor Corp.

Strategy

Minus 19

For **Minus** 19, subtract 20 and add 1.

Turn **Minus** 19 problems into **Minus** 20 problems.

$$80 - 19 \rightarrow 80 \overset{60}{- 20} + 1 = 61$$

Try it.

70 − 19 → _____

90 − 19 → _____

55 − 19 → _____

68 − 19 → _____

Strategy

Minus 99

For **Minus** 99, subtract 100 and add 1.

Turn **Minus** 99 problems into **Minus** 100 problems.

$$160 - 99 \rightarrow 160 \overset{60}{- 100} + 1 = 61$$

Try it.

200 − 99 → _____

300 − 99 → _____

350 − 99 → _____

450 − 99 → _____

Strategy

Subtract in Small Steps

It's easier to subtract from a multiple of 10. Use this strategy to "subtract down" to 10 or a multiple of 10 (20, 30, 40, and so on).

Look at the first number (the minuend from which you are subtracting).
Decide how much to subtract to reach 10 or a multiple of 10.
Subtract that amount.
Subtract the remaining amount.

$15 - 6 = ?$

Step 1: Split **6** into <u>5 and 1</u>.

Step 2: $(15 - 5) - 1$ (don't forget the 1)

Step 3: $10 - 1$

Solve it! 9

Subtract in small steps.

Split 4 into
−3 and −1

$13 - 4 =$ _____

$34 - 6 =$ _____

$21 - 5 =$ _____

$31 - 6 =$ _____

Split 5 into
−2 and −3

$22 - 5 =$ _____

$24 - 7 =$ _____

$44 - 8 =$ _____

$22 - 4 =$ _____

Split 8 into
−6 and −2

$26 - 8 =$ _____

$23 - 5 =$ _____

$25 - 7 =$ _____

$33 - 7 =$ _____

Building Math Fluency • EMC 3036 • © Evan-Moor Corp.

Name _____

Many Ways to Subtract

$$34 - 9 = ?$$

Think about which strategy makes sense to you.

See 9. Think 10.
I subtract 10 and add 1.

$$34 - 9 = 34 - 10 + 1$$
$$= 24 + 1$$
$$= 25$$

Subtract in Small Steps
I split 9 into 4 and 5.

$$34 - 9 = 34 - 4 - 5$$
$$= 30 - 5$$
$$= 25$$

Think about the problems. Choose a strategy. Show your work.

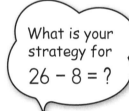

What is your strategy for $26 - 8 = ?$

My strategy was _____.

What is your strategy for $18 - 9 = ?$

My strategy was _____.

Name _____

Name That Strategy

Strategy Names

Count Back   Doubles   Minus 10   Minus 9   Tens Partners   ~~Think Addition~~

Solve the problems.
Write the strategy name.

Strategy name	Strategy name	Strategy name
Think Addition		
22 – 19 = _____	10 – 4 = _____	14 – 7 = _____
40 – 36 = _____	10 – 3 = _____	16 – 8 = _____
15 – 12 = _____	10 – 9 = _____	18 – 9 = _____
23 – 18 = _____	10 – 8 = _____	8 – 4 = _____
31 – 28 = _____	10 – 7 = _____	12 – 6 = _____
21 – 15 = _____	10 – 6 = _____	6 – 3 = _____

Strategy name	Strategy name	Strategy name
16 – 10 = _____	16 – 9 = _____	11 – 2 = _____
14 – 10 = _____	14 – 9 = _____	22 – 3 = _____
23 – 10 = _____	23 – 9 = _____	18 – 1 = _____
25 – 10 = _____	25 – 9 = _____	12 – 3 = _____
34 – 10 = _____	34 – 9 = _____	19 – 1 = _____
47 – 10 = _____	47 – 9 = _____	21 – 2 = _____

Fact Power Skill Builders

Skill Builders -4, -5, -6

Think about subtraction strategies. Solve.

-4	-5	-6
10 − 4 = _____	10 − 5 = _____	10 − 6 = _____
6 − 4 = _____	8 − 5 = _____	6 − 6 = _____
9 − 4 = _____	9 − 5 = _____	9 − 6 = _____
7 − 4 = _____	7 − 5 = _____	7 − 6 = _____
8 − 4 = _____	6 − 5 = _____	8 − 6 = _____
5 − 4 = _____	12 − 5 = _____	11 − 6 = _____
11 − 4 = _____	15 − 5 = _____	12 − 6 = _____
12 − 4 = _____	11 − 5 = _____	13 − 6 = _____
15 − 4 = _____	16 − 5 = _____	15 − 6 = _____
18 − 4 = _____	14 − 5 = _____	18 − 6 = _____
16 − 4 = _____	19 − 5 = _____	16 − 6 = _____
14 − 4 = _____	18 − 5 = _____	14 − 6 = _____
20 − 4 = _____	13 − 5 = _____	20 − 6 = _____

Name _____

Skill Builders -7, -8, -9

Use subtraction strategies to solve.

-7	-8	-9
10 − 7 = _____	16 − 8 = _____	10 − 9 = _____
14 − 7 = _____	8 − 8 = _____	20 − 9 = _____
9 − 7 = _____	9 − 8 = _____	9 − 9 = _____
7 − 7 = _____	10 − 8 = _____	11 − 9 = _____
11 − 7 = _____	12 − 8 = _____	18 − 9 = _____
8 − 7 = _____	14 − 8 = _____	17 − 9 = _____
17 − 7 = _____	15 − 8 = _____	11 − 9 = _____
12 − 7 = _____	11 − 8 = _____	12 − 9 = _____
13 − 7 = _____	20 − 8 = _____	15 − 9 = _____
20 − 7 = _____	17 − 8 = _____	13 − 9 = _____
18 − 7 = _____	18 − 8 = _____	16 − 9 = _____
19 − 7 = _____	19 − 8 = _____	14 − 9 = _____
15 − 7 = _____	13 − 8 = _____	19 − 9 = _____

     Building Math Fluency • EMC 3036 • © Evan-Moor Corp.

Name _____

Pocket Companions

Here's one way to learn a difficult math fact:

- Write it down and put it in your pocket.
- Take it out when you have some free time—while walking the dog or riding in the car.
- Practice it in your mind.

Here's an example:

I keep forgetting 13 − 8 = ?
I'll write it down and put it in my pocket.

Front
13, 8, 5

Back
8 + 5 = 13
5 + 8 = 13
13 − 5 = 8
13 − 8 = 5

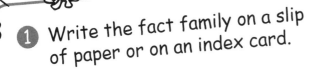

1 Write the fact family on a slip of paper or on an index card.

2 Carry the paper with you. Think about the fact family. (This technique works best using one pocket companion at a time.)

3 When you have mastered the fact family, select another set of numbers to put into your pocket and to practice.

Subtraction Skill Builders

Name _____

Subtraction by Design

Use subtraction strategies to solve each problem.
Color as directed in the chart below.

18 – 9	20 – 16	12 – 6	12 – 4	9 – 5	13 – 7	14 – 6
20 – 14	17 – 8	15 – 10	20 – 13	15 – 6	8 – 3	16 – 9
12 – 8	9 – 3	16 – 8	10 – 5	16 – 10	11 – 2	18 – 13
14 – 5	12 – 7	10 – 4	18 – 10	8 – 4	10 – 3	20 – 11
17 – 10	13 – 4	11 – 6	11 – 4	20 – 12	10 – 6	12 – 5
16 – 11	14 – 7	13 – 5	11 – 7	9 – 2	16 – 7	20 – 15
15 – 7	16 – 12	15 – 8	17 – 9	9 – 4	8 – 1	19 – 10

Difference	Color
4 or 5	green
6 or 7	yellow
8 or 9	blue

Building Math Fluency • EMC 3036 • © Evan-Moor Corp.

Teaching Multiplication Strategies

Pages 53–83 present practice with multiplication strategies that promote computational fluency and fact mastery. (A blackline of the multiplication table is on page 159.) Multiplication facts are introduced sequentially with the exception of Times 10, which is presented after Times 4 because Times 10 facts are easy to learn and important to subsequent strategies.

As you work through the multiplication strategy pages, continue to stress the commutative property of multiplication. Students should recognize that if they need to count by groups to solve multiplication problems, it may be more efficient to count by one factor than the other. For example, a problem such as 9×4 (9 groups of 4) is easier to count than 4×9 (4 groups of 9).

Understanding multiplication is enhanced through the exploration of number relationships, the discovery of patterns in and among multiples, and the establishment of personal "anchor facts," most commonly: Times 2, Times 5, and Times 10.

Addition   Here are two ways to use addition to solve multiplication:

Repetitive Addition
Example: $3 \times 8 = ?$

Solution: $8 + 8 + 8 = 24$

Skip Count
Example: $7 \times 5 = ?$

Solution: Count by fives 7 times:
5, 10, 15, 20, 25, 30, 35

Anchor Facts   Use well-known multiplication facts to solve unknowns. The 2s facts, 5s facts, and 10s facts are particularly useful for solving the more difficult Times 7, Times 9, and Times 12 problems.

Times 7 Strategy

Times 7 = Times 5 + Times 2

Example: $7 \times 8 = ?$
      Well, I know:
      (5×8) and $(2 \times 8) =$
             $40 + 16 = 56$

Times 9 Strategy

Times 9 = Times 10 – Times 1

Example: $9 \times 6 = ?$
      I do know:
      $10 \times 6 = 60$
      and $60 - 6 = 54$.

Times 12 Strategy

Times 12 = Times 10 + Times 2

Example: $12 \times 11 = ?$
      I can do:
      (12×10) and $(12 \times 1) =$
             $120 + 12 = 132$

Unknown Facts

$7 \times 6 = ?$ Hmm, I know $6 \times 6 = 36$, so another 6 makes 42.

$4 \times 9 = ?$ I know 2×9 is 18, so double this and I get 36.

$12 \times 13 = ?$ Let's see, $10 \times 13 = 130$ and $2 \times 13 = 26$, so $130 + 26 = 156$.

$19 \times 6 = ?$ Well, $20 \times 6 = 120$ and $120 - 6 = 114$.

Multiplication Strategies

Times 0	0 Times a number is always 0.
Times 1	Times 1 equals the number.
Times 2	Times 2 is double the number.
Times 3	Times 3 is the number tripled. Double the number and add one more group.
Times 4	Times 4 is double Times 2. Times 4 = Times 2 + Times 2. Double the number and double again.
Times 5	Times 5 is like counting nickels. Times 5 is half of Times 10. Times 5 = Times 10 ÷ 2.
Times 6	Times 6 is double Times 3. Times 6 = Times 3 + Times 3. Times 6 = Times 5 + Times 1.
Times 7	Turn Times 7 into smaller multiplication facts: Times 7 = Times 5 + Times 2.
Times 8	Times 8 is double Times 4. Times 8 = Times 4 + Times 4.
Times 9	See Times 9. Think Times 10. Think Times 10 and subtract one group. Times 9 = Times 10 − Times 1.
Times 10	Times 10 increases a number tenfold. Put a 0 in the ones place to increase its value.
Times 11	Single-digit factors Times 11 make double-digit products. (3 x 11 = 33) Times 11 is one group more than Times 10. Times 11 = Times 10 + Times 1.
Times 12	Times 12 = Times 10 + Times 2. Times 12 = Times 6 + Times 6.

Building Math Fluency • EMC 3036 • © Evan-Moor Corp.

Strategy

Equal Groups

Use multiplication to total items that come in equal groups, or sets.

Multiplication counts **equal groups** of items.
Complete each chart with the missing item.
The first chart is done for you.

Write	3 x 12
Say	three groups of twelve
Draw	

Write	2 x 6
Say	
Draw	

Write	4 x 5
Say	four groups of five
Draw	

Write	
Say	three groups of four
Draw	

Strategy

Commutative Property

Change the order of the factors, and the product stays the same.

factor factor
$$8 \times 3 = 24 \longleftrightarrow 3 \times 8 = 24$$
product   product
factor factor

Write the Turn Around fact for each problem.

3 x 5 = _____   4 x 9 = _____   6 x 2 = _____

7 x 8 = _____   1 x 12 = _____   3 x 9 = _____

Times 2
Times 3

Name _____

Times 2 is double the number.
Times 3 is double the number plus one more group of the number.

Times 2 is double the number.
Complete the chart.

Times 2	Doubles Fact	Answer
2 x 6	6 + 6	
2 x 9		
2 x 8		
2 x 11		
2 x 7		
2 x 12		

Times 3 is double the number plus one more group of the number.
Times 3 = Times 2 + Times 1.

Example: $3 \times 6 = (6 + 6) + 6$
$= 12 + 6$
$= 18$

Complete the chart.

Times 3	Doubles Fact + _____	Answer
3 x 9	(9 + 9) + 9	
3 x 8		
3 x 11		
3 x 7		
3 x 12		

Building Math Fluency • EMC 3036 • © Evan-Moor Corp.

Name _____

Times 0, 1, 2, 3

Times 0 is zero.

$0 \times 3 =$ _____ $0 \times 7 =$ _____ $0 \times 12 =$ _____ $0 \times 15 =$ _____

Times 1 equals the number.

$1 \times 3 =$ _____ $1 \times 7 =$ _____ $1 \times 12 =$ _____ $1 \times 15 =$ _____

Times 2 doubles the number.

$2 \times 3 =$ _____ $2 \times 7 =$ _____ $2 \times 12 =$ _____ $2 \times 15 =$ _____

Times 3 triples the number.

$3 \times 3 =$ _____ $3 \times 7 =$ _____ $3 \times 12 =$ _____ $3 \times 15 =$ _____

Explain how **Times 2** facts help solve **Times 3** facts.
Then give an example.

_____

_____

_____

_____

Strategy

Times 4

Times 4 is Times 2 + Times 2.

Times 4 is four sets of the number.
Put the four sets in two groups for easier computation.

Four sets: $4 \times 6 =$ ▓▓▓ ▓▓▓ ▓▓▓ ▓▓▓ $= 24$
$ 6 \; + \; 6 \; + \; 6 \; + \; 6$

Two groups: $4 \times 6 =$ ▓▓▓ ▓▓▓ ▓▓▓ ▓▓▓ $= 24$
$ 12 + 12$

Or think of it like this:

$$4 \times 6 = \overset{12}{(6 + 6)} + \overset{12}{(6 + 6)} = 24$$

Put the four sets in two groups for easier computation.
Circle the two groups and solve.

$4 \times 5 = (5 + 5) + (5 + 5) =$ _____

$4 \times 7 = 7 + 7 + 7 + 7 =$ _____

$4 \times 8 = 8 + 8 + 8 + 8 =$ _____

$4 \times 9 = 9 + 9 + 9 + 9 =$ _____

$4 \times 12 = 12 + 12 + 12 + 12 =$ _____

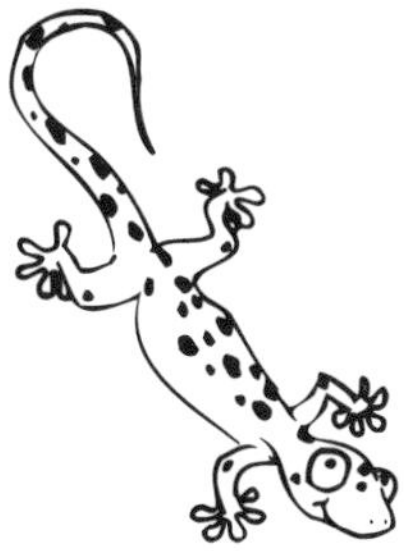

Mixed Strategies Practice

Name ______________________________

Times 2, 3, 4

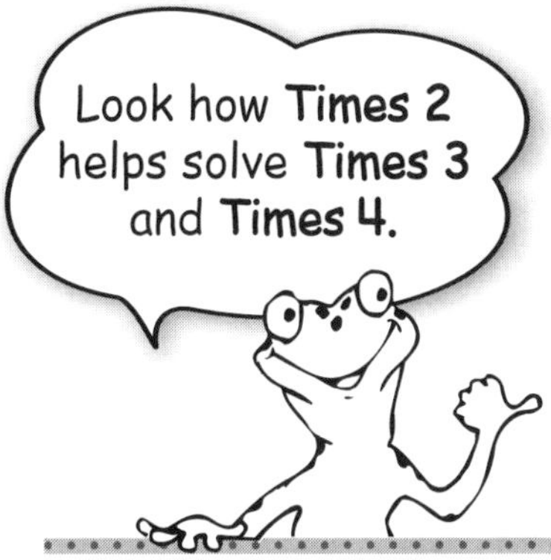

Look how Times 2 helps solve Times 3 and Times 4.

Times 3

3 x 7 = ?

Think **Times 2 + Times 1**

2 x 7 = 14

1 x 7 = 7

so

3 x 7 = 14 + 7

= 21

Times 4

4 x 7 = ?

Think **Times 2 + Times 2**

2 x 7 = 14

2 x 7 = 14

so

4 x 7 = 14 + 14

= 28

Multiply	**x2** Times 2	**x3** Times 2 + Times 1	**x4** Times 2 + Times 2
0	0		
1	2		
2	4		
3			
4			
5			
6			
7			
8			
9			
10			
11			
12			

Times 10

Name _____

Times 10 increases a number tenfold.

Count the 10s. Label the rows.

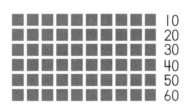
```
10
20
30
40
50
60
```

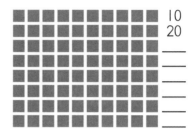
```
10
20
___
___
___
___
___
```

6 x 10 = _____   8 x 10 = _____

Use **Times 10** to solve the problems.

10 x 1 = _____   10 x 5 = _____   10 x 9 = _____

10 x 2 = _____   10 x 6 = _____   10 x 10 = _____

10 x 3 = _____   10 x 7 = _____   10 x 11 = _____

10 x 4 = _____   10 x 8 = _____   10 x 12 = _____

```
   14          15          16          17          18
x  10       x  10       x  10       x  10       x  10
_____       _____       _____       _____       _____
```

```
   19          20          30          40         100
x  10       x  10       x  10       x  10       x  10
_____       _____       _____       _____       _____
```

Building Math Fluency • EMC 3036 • © Evan-Moor Corp.

Name _____

Times 5 is half of Times 10.

To solve **Times 5**, divide the Times 10 product in half.

$$5 \times 12 = ?$$

$$10 \times 12 = \underline{120}$$

so $5 \times 12 = \underline{120} \div \underline{2} = \underline{60}$

Try it.

$$5 \times 14 = ?$$

$$10 \times 14 = \underline{}$$

so $5 \times 14 = \underline{} \div \underline{} = \underline{}$

$$5 \times 16 = ?$$

$$10 \times 16 = \underline{}$$

so $5 \times 16 = \underline{} \div \underline{} = \underline{}$

Complete the chart.

Halve the product.

Multiply	x10	x5
1		
2		
3		
4		
5		
6		
7		
8		
9		
10		
11		
12		
13		
14		
15		
16		
17		
18		
19		
20		

What do you notice?

_____

_____

Strategy

Times 5

Times 5 is half of **Times 10**.

Times 5 is half of **Times 10**.
Dividing in half is easy if you know Doubles facts.

4 + 4 = 8, so half of _8_ is _4_.

40 + 40 = 80, so half of _80_ is _40_.

6 + 6 = 12, so half of ___ is ___.

60 + 60 = 120, so half of ___ is ___.

7 + 7 = 14, so half of ___ is ___.

70 + 70 = 140, so half of ___ is ___.

Times 5 can be solved by doing **Times 10** and then dividing in half.

5 x 12 = ?

10 x 12 = _120_

so 5 x 12 = _120 ÷ 2 =_

5 x 16 = ?

10 x 16 = _____

so 5 x 16 = ____ ÷ 2 =

5 x 14 = ?

10 x 14 = _____

so 5 x 14 = ____ ÷ 2 =

5 x 18 = ?

10 x 18 = _____

so 5 x 18 = ____ ÷ 2 =

····· **Strategy** ·····

Times 6

Times 6 is counting by sixes.

Solve the **Times 6** facts.

1 x 6 = _____ ☐☐☐☐☐☐ 6

2 x 6 = _____ [grid] 6
12

3 x 6 = _____ [grid] 6
12
18

4 x 6 = _____ [grid]

5 x 6 = _____ [grid]

6 x 6 = _____ [grid]

7 x 6 = _____ [grid]

8 x 6 = _____ [grid]

9 x 6 = _____ [grid]

10 x 6 = _____ [grid]

11 x 6 = _____

12 x 6 = _____

Multiplication **61**

Strategy

Times 6

Times 6 is double **Times 3**.

Times 3 Facts	Double the 3 Facts

$3 \times 4 = $ _____   Double → $6 \times 4 = $ _____

Solve **Times 3** and **Times 6**.

$3 \times 4 = $ _____	$3 \times 8 = $ _____
$6 \times 4 = $ _____	$6 \times 8 = $ _____
$3 \times 5 = $ _____	$3 \times 9 = $ _____
$6 \times 5 = $ _____	$6 \times 9 = $ _____
$3 \times 6 = $ _____	$3 \times 11 = $ _____
$6 \times 6 = $ _____	$6 \times 11 = $ _____
$3 \times 7 = $ _____	$3 \times 12 = $ _____
$6 \times 7 = $ _____	$6 \times 12 = $ _____

Strategy

Times 7

Times 7 can be solved with multiplication facts you know.
Times 7 = Times 5 + Times 2.

One way to think about **Times 7** is to imagine tally marks for each group of 7.
Seven tally marks make a group of 5 tallies and 2 tallies.

3 × 7 is:

See three groups of 7 tally marks.
Count the 5s and add on the 2s.
3 × 7 = 15 + 6 = 21

For six groups of 7 tallies:
Count the 5s.
Add on the 2s.

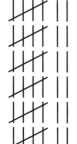

____ + ____ = ____

6 × 7 = ____

For eight groups of 7 tallies:
Count the 5s.
Add on the 2s.

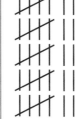

____ + ____ = ____

8 × 7 = ____

For seven groups of 7 tallies:
Count the 5s.
Add on the 2s.

____ + ____ = ____

7 × 7 = ____

For nine groups of 7 tallies:
Count the 5s.
Add on the 2s.

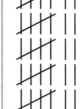

____ + ____ = ____

9 × 7 = ____

Strategy

Times 7

Times 7 can be solved with multiplication facts you know.

$$7 \times 6 = 7 \overset{35}{\times} 5 \text{ and } 7 \overset{7}{\times} 1 = 42$$

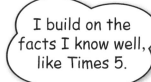

I build on the facts I know well, like Times 5.

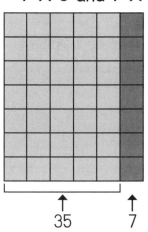

$\uparrow$ 35 $\uparrow$ 7

Solve the problems.

$$7 \times 7 = 7 \overset{35}{\times} 5 \text{ and } 7 \overset{14}{\times} 2 = \text{_____}$$

$$7 \times 8 = 7 \overset{35}{\times} 5 \text{ and } 7 \overset{21}{\times} 3 = \text{_____}$$

$$7 \times 9 = 7 \overset{35}{\times} 5 \text{ and } 7 \overset{28}{\times} 4 = \text{_____}$$

$$7 \times 10 = 7 \overset{35}{\times} 5 \text{ and } 7 \overset{35}{\times} 5 = \text{_____}$$

Memory Aid

To remember **7 × 8 = 56**,
place digits in consecutive order (5, 6, 7, 8)
and insert the symbols **=** and **X**.

$$56 = 7 \times 8$$

Name _____

Times 6, Times 7

Write the multiplication equation for each picture.
Match the equation to the Turn Around fact.

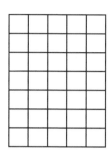

_____ X _____ = _____   •

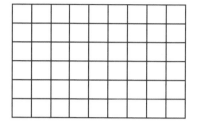

•   _____ X _____ = _____

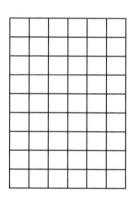

_____ X _____ = _____   •

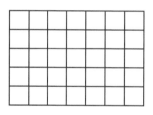

•   _____ X _____ = _____

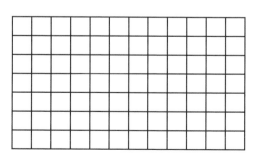

_____ X _____ = _____   •

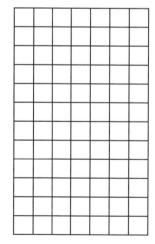

•   _____ X _____ = _____

Strategy

Times 8

Times 8 is counting by eights.

Solve the **Times 8** facts.

1 x 8 = _____

2 x 8 = _____

3 x 8 = _____

4 x 8 = _____

5 x 8 = _____

6 x 8 = _____

7 x 8 = _____

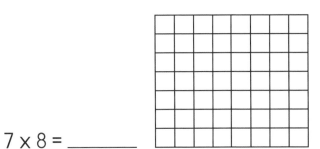

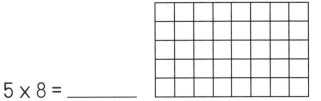

8 x 8 = _____

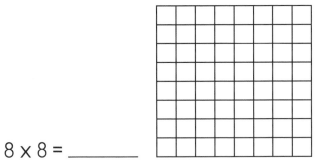

9 x 8 = _____

10 x 8 = _____

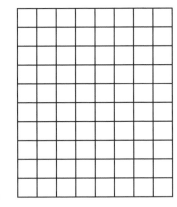

11 x 8 = _____

12 x 8 = _____

Building Math Fluency • EMC 3036 • © Evan-Moor Corp.

Strategy

Times 8

Times 8 is double **Times 4**.

Times 4 Facts	**Times 8 Facts**

4 x 3 = _____

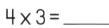

   Times 4

Double →

8 x 3 = _____

Times 4

Times 4

Solve **Times 4** and **Times 8**.

4 x 4 = _____   4 x 8 = _____

8 x 4 = _____   8 x 8 = _____

4 x 5 = _____   4 x 9 = _____

8 x 5 = _____   8 x 9 = _____

4 x 6 = _____   4 x 11 = _____

8 x 6 = _____   8 x 11 = _____

4 x 7 = _____   4 x 12 = _____

8 x 7 = _____   8 x 12 = _____

Name _____

Double the Product

Complete the multiplication charts.

Multiply	x3	x6
1		
2		
3		
4		
5		
6		
7		
8		
9		
10		
11		
12		

Multiply	x4	x8
1		
2		
3		
4		
5		
6		
7		
8		
9		
10		
11		
12		

Examine the completed charts.
What patterns do you notice? _____

_____

Building Math Fluency • EMC 3036 • © Evan-Moor Corp.

Strategy

Times 9

Times 9 is counting by nines.

Solve the **Times 9** facts.

I x 9 = _____   6 x 9 = _____

2 x 9 = _____   7 x 9 = _____

3 x 9 = _____   8 x 9 = _____

4 x 9 = _____   9 x 9 = _____

5 x 9 = _____   10 x 9 = _____

What patterns can you find in the products?

_____

_____

_____

Solve.

I I x 9 = _____   12 x 9 = _____   13 x 9 = _____

Strategy

Times 9

Times 9 = Times 10 − Times 1.

$$4 \times 9 = ?$$

For 4 x 9, do 4 x 10. Then subtract 4.

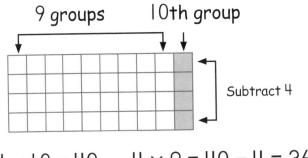

9 groups   10th group

Subtract 4

$$4 \times 10 = 40 \qquad 4 \times 9 = 40 - 4 = 36$$

Try **Times 9**. Solve the parentheses first.

$$7 \times 9 = ?$$

Think Times 10.
Then subtract Times 1.

$7 \times 9 = (7 \times 10) - (7 \times 1) =$ _____

$$9 \times 9 = ?$$

Think Times 10.
Then subtract Times 1.

$9 \times 9 = (9 \times 10) - (9 \times 1) =$ _____

$$6 \times 9 = ?$$

Think Times 10.
Then subtract Times 1.

$6 \times 9 = (6 \times 10) - (6 \times 1) =$ _____

Name _____

Square Numbers

When both factors are the same, the product is called a **square number**.
Draw and label each square number on the grid. The first two are done for you.

1×1   2×2   3×3   4×4   5×5   6×6   7×7   8×8   9×9

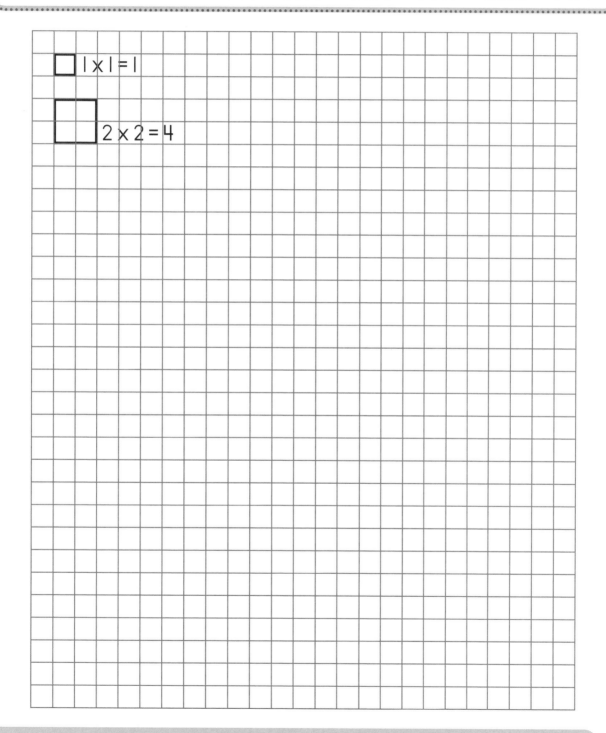

□ 1 × 1 = 1

□ 2 × 2 = 4

Times 11

Name _____

Build on **Times 10** to solve **Times 11**.

Single-Digit Factors

Solve the **Times 11** facts.

2 x 11 = _____   6 x 11 = _____

3 x 11 = _____   7 x 11 = _____

4 x 11 = _____   8 x 11 = _____

5 x 11 = _____   9 x 11 = _____

What is the pattern? _____

Double-Digit Factors

For double-digit factors, build on **Times 10** facts.
Multiply the number by 10, and add one more group of the number.
Solve the parentheses first.

11 x 11 = (11 x 10) + 11 = _____

12 x 11 = (12 x 10) + 12 = _____

13 x 11 = (13 x 10) + 13 = _____

14 x 11 = (14 x 10) + 14 = _____

15 x 11 = (15 x 10) + 15 = _____

16 x 11 = (16 x 10) + 16 = _____

Building Math Fluency • EMC 3036 • © Evan-Moor Corp.

Strategy

Times 12

Build on **Times 10**
to solve **Times 12**.

Solve the **Times 12** facts.
Count by 12s.

1 x 12 = _____   7 x 12 = _____

2 x 12 = _____   8 x 12 = _____

3 x 12 = _____   9 x 12 = _____

4 x 12 = _____   10 x 12 = _____

5 x 12 = _____   11 x 12 = _____

6 x 12 = _____   12 x 12 = _____

Build on Times 10 Facts

Multiply the number by 10, and add two more groups of the number.
Solve the parentheses first.

$$12 \times 12 = (12 \times 10) + 12 + 12 = \underline{\hspace{5cm}}$$
(120 above 12×10, 24 above +12+12)

$$13 \times 12 = (13 \times 10) + 13 + 13 = \underline{\hspace{5cm}}$$

$$14 \times 12 = (14 \times 10) + 14 + 14 = \underline{\hspace{5cm}}$$

$$15 \times 12 = (15 \times 10) + 15 + 15 = \underline{\hspace{5cm}}$$

$$16 \times 12 = (16 \times 10) + 16 + 16 = \underline{\hspace{5cm}}$$

Name _____

Many Ways to Multiply

$$4 \times 9 = ?$$

Think about which strategy makes sense to you.

I know two 9s is 18, so four 9s is 36.

$$2 \times 9 = 18$$
$$4 \times 9 = 18 + 18$$
$$= 36$$

I like 10s facts, so I do Times 10 and subtract.

$$4 \times 10 = 40$$
$$4 \times 9 = 40 - 4$$
$$= 36$$

Think about the problems. Choose a strategy. Show your work.

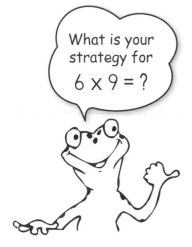

What is your strategy for

$$6 \times 9 = ?$$

My strategy was _____.

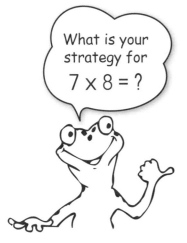

What is your strategy for

$$7 \times 8 = ?$$

My strategy was _____.

Building Math Fluency • EMC 3036 • © Evan-Moor Corp.

Mixed Strategies Practice

100 Products

Complete the chart.

X	1	2	3	4	5	6	7	8	9	10
1										
2										
3										
4										
5										
6										
7										
8										
9										
10										

Square numbers have the same factors (1 x 1, 2 x 2, 3 x 3, etc.).
Shade the boxes with square products in yellow.

Challenge: Which two square numbers total 100?

☐ + ☐ = 100

Name _____

Skip Count by 2, 3, and 4

Skip Count to practice multiplication facts.
Include skip counting in regular math work-outs. Here's how:

- Write down the numbers.
- Say them out loud.
- Tap or clap in rhythm.

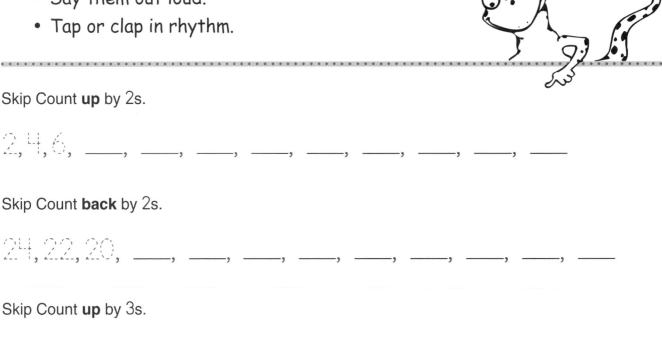

Skip Count **up** by 2s.

2, 4, 6, ___, ___, ___, ___, ___, ___, ___, ___, ___

Skip Count **back** by 2s.

24, 22, 20, ___, ___, ___, ___, ___, ___, ___, ___, ___

Skip Count **up** by 3s.

3, 6, 9, ___, ___, ___, ___, ___, ___, ___, ___, ___

Skip Count **back** by 3s.

36, 33, 30, ___, ___, ___, ___, ___, ___, ___, ___, ___

Skip Count **up** by 4s.

4, 8, ___, ___, ___, ___, ___, ___, ___, ___, ___, ___

Skip Count **back** by 4s.

48, 44, ___, ___, ___, ___, ___, ___, ___, ___, ___, ___

Name _____

Skip Count by 5, 6, and 7

Skip Count to practice multiplication facts.
Include skip counting in regular math work-outs. Here's how:

- Write down the numbers.
- Say them out loud.
- Tap or clap in rhythm.

Skip Count **up** by 5s.

5, 10, ____, ____, ____, ____, ____, ____, ____, ____, ____, ____

Skip Count **back** by 5s.

60, 55, ____, ____, ____, ____, ____, ____, ____, ____, ____, ____

Skip Count **up** by 6s.

6, 12, ____, ____, ____, ____, ____, ____, ____, ____, ____, ____

Skip Count **back** by 6s.

72, 66, ____, ____, ____, ____, ____, ____, ____, ____, ____, ____

Skip Count **up** by 7s.

7, 14, ____, ____, ____, ____, ____, ____, ____, ____, ____, ____

Skip Count **back** by 7s.

84, 77, ____, ____, ____, ____, ____, ____, ____, ____, ____, ____

Name _____

Skip Count by 8, 9, and 12

Skip Count to practice multiplication facts.
Include skip counting in regular math work-outs. Here's how:
- Write down the numbers.
- Say them out loud.
- Tap or clap in rhythm.

Skip Count **up** by 8s.

8, 16, ____, ____, ____, ____, ____, ____, ____, ____, ____, ____

Skip Count **back** by 8s.

96, 88, ____, ____, ____, ____, ____, ____, ____, ____, ____, ____

Skip Count **up** by 9s.

9, 18, ____, ____, ____, ____, ____, ____, ____, ____, ____, ____

Skip Count **back** by 9s.

108, 99, ____, ____, ____, ____, ____, ____, ____, ____, ____, ____

Skip Count **up** by 12s.

12, 24, ____, ____, ____, ____, ____, ____, ____, ____, ____, ____

Skip Count **back** by 12s.

144, 132, ____, ____, ____, ____, ____, ____, ____, ____, ____, ____

**Fact Power
Skill Builders**

Name _____

Math Rhymes

Rhymes can help you to remember math facts.

Nine times nine is a lot of <u>fun</u>.
The answer is eighty-<u>one</u>.

$9 \times 9 = 81$

Fun rhymes with **one**.

Write rhymes for only your hardest math facts.
Otherwise, you'll have too many rhymes to remember.
Use this formula if you like. The second and fourth lines end in rhyming words.

1. Number times number

2. _____.

3. The answer is

4. _____.

Words That Rhyme with Numbers

one	two	three	four	five	six	seven	eight	nine
fun	blue	glee	door	hive	fix	heaven	bait	dine
ton	crew	free	core	jive	bricks	Kevin	wait	fine
bun	glue	see/sea	more	skydive	chicks	Devon	skate	shrine
run	hullabaloo	tea	roar	drive	mix/nix	Evan	late	whine
son	shoe	M.D.	score	arrive	tricks	eleven	great	line

Name _____

Skill Builders x4, x5, x6

Use your strategies to multiply.

x4	x5	x6
1 x 4 = _____	10 x 5 = _____	2 x 6 = _____
2 x 4 = _____	3 x 5 = _____	4 x 6 = _____
4 x 4 = _____	5 x 5 = _____	5 x 6 = _____
5 x 4 = _____	2 x 5 = _____	3 x 6 = _____
8 x 4 = _____	4 x 5 = _____	6 x 6 = _____
7 x 4 = _____	6 x 5 = _____	7 x 6 = _____
10 x 4 = _____	7 x 5 = _____	8 x 6 = _____
12 x 4 = _____	9 x 5 = _____	9 x 6 = _____
3 x 4 = _____	8 x 5 = _____	10 x 6 = _____
6 x 4 = _____	11 x 5 = _____	11 x 6 = _____
9 x 4 = _____	12 x 5 = _____	12 x 6 = _____
11 x 4 = _____	1 x 5 = _____	1 x 6 = _____

Building Math Fluency • EMC 3036 • © Evan-Moor Corp.

Name _____

Skill Builders x7, x8, x9

Use your strategies to multiply.

x7	x8	x9
1 x 7 = _____	2 x 8 = _____	1 x 9 = _____
2 x 7 = _____	3 x 8 = _____	2 x 9 = _____
3 x 7 = _____	5 x 8 = _____	5 x 9 = _____
4 x 7 = _____	7 x 8 = _____	10 x 9 = _____
10 x 7 = _____	4 x 8 = _____	9 x 9 = _____
9 x 7 = _____	8 x 8 = _____	3 x 9 = _____
11 x 7 = _____	1 x 8 = _____	4 x 9 = _____
5 x 7 = _____	6 x 8 = _____	8 x 9 = _____
6 x 7 = _____	9 x 8 = _____	6 x 9 = _____
7 x 7 = _____	10 x 8 = _____	7 x 9 = _____
8 x 7 = _____	11 x 8 = _____	11 x 9 = _____
12 x 7 = _____	12 x 8 = _____	12 x 9 = _____

Name _____

Skill Builders x10, x11, x12

Use your strategies to multiply.

x10	x11	x12
1 x 10 = _____	2 x 11 = _____	1 x 12 = _____
2 x 10 = _____	3 x 11 = _____	2 x 12 = _____
3 x 10 = _____	5 x 11 = _____	5 x 12 = _____
4 x 10 = _____	7 x 11 = _____	10 x 12 = _____
10 x 10 = _____	4 x 11 = _____	9 x 12 = _____
9 x 10 = _____	8 x 11 = _____	3 x 12 = _____
11 x 10 = _____	1 x 11 = _____	4 x 12 = _____
5 x 10 = _____	6 x 11 = _____	8 x 12 = _____
6 x 10 = _____	9 x 11 = _____	6 x 12 = _____
7 x 10 = _____	10 x 11 = _____	7 x 12 = _____
8 x 10 = _____	11 x 11 = _____	11 x 12 = _____
12 x 10 = _____	12 x 11 = _____	12 x 12 = _____

Building Math Fluency • EMC 3036 • © Evan-Moor Corp.

Name _____

Multiplication by Design

Use addition strategies to solve each problem.
Color as directed in the chart below.

3 x 9	15 x 4	6 x 3	10 x 10	2 x 9	6 x 5	8 x 8
5 x 7	7 x 9	11 x 6	4 x 8	9 x 10	9 x 4	6 x 7
12 x 2	7 x 10	2 x 3	4 x 1	5 x 2	11 x 8	3 x 7
9 x 8	4 x 4	1 x 7	5 x 5	10 x 0	8 x 2	8 x 9
5 x 3	50 x 2	4 x 2	9 x 1	3 x 3	8 x 10	6 x 4
7 x 4	7 x 8	11 x 9	2 x 7	11 x 7	6 x 8	5 x 9
6 x 6	9 x 6	4 x 5	9 x 9	3 x 4	7 x 7	4 x 8

Product	Color
between 0 and 10	red
between 11 and 25	yellow
between 26 and 65	blue
between 66 and 100	green

Teaching Division Strategies

Pages 86–104 present practice with division strategies that are introductory in nature and that are presented primarily as a means to reinforce multiplication concepts. These strategies focus on key number patterns and number relationships to promote fact mastery and build computational fluency.

To divide means to share items equally; to separate quantities into "fair shares."

$$\overset{\text{dividend}}{\underset{}{16}} \div \overset{\text{divisor}}{\underset{}{8}} = \underset{\text{quotient}}{2}$$

Basic Properties of Division

0 divided by a number is 0.

$0 \div N = 0$

A number divided by itself is 1.

$N \div N = 1$

A number divided by 1 equals the number.

$N \div 1 = N$

Note: **N ÷ 0** can not be done. If **N ÷ 0 = A** was possible, then it would follow that **A X 0 = N**, but this is <u>not</u> true. Another way to view this is that you can't divide a quantity into groups of 0.

Division Strategies

Use Doubles Facts

$12 \div 2 = 6$ because two sixes make 12.

$18 \div 2 = 9$ because two nines make 18.

Think Multiplication

24 ÷ 6 = ?

Think: 6 X *what* = 24. The answer is 4.

$24 \div 6 = 4$

54 ÷ 9 = ?

Think: 9 X *what* = 54. The answer is 6.

$54 \div 9 = 6$

Building Math Fluency • EMC 3036 • © Evan-Moor Corp.

Division Strategies

Division of 0	0 divided by any number is 0. $$0 \div 6 = 0$$ If there are 0 things, there is nothing to divide into groups.
	Division by 0 is **not** possible. $$8 \div 0 =$$ You can't divide 8 things into 0 groups. That makes no sense.
A Number Divided by Itself	A number divided by itself is 1. $$3 \div 3 = 1 \qquad 89 \div 89 = 1$$
Division by 1	A number divided by 1 equals the number. $$3 \div 1 = 3 \qquad 89 \div 1 = 89$$
Division by 2	A number divided by 2 is half the number. Use Doubles facts to solve Division by 2. $$8 \div 2 = ?$$
Division by 3–12	Use related multiplication to solve division problems. For example: $$40 \div 5 = ?$$ Think: $5 \times$ *what* $= 40$ $$5 \times 8 = 40,$$ so $40 \div 5 = 8$.

Name _____

Equal Groups

Divide the amount into equal groups.

$12 \div 2$ means:
12 items divided into 2 equal groups.

$$12 \div 2 = 6$$

● ● ● ● ● ● | ● ● ● ● ● ●

$12 \div 3$ means:
12 divided into 3 equal groups.

$12 \div 4$ means:
12 divided into 4 equal groups.

$12 \div 6$ means:
12 divided into 6 equal groups.

Complete the sentence. Draw a picture to match the equation.

$8 \div 2$ means: _____ .

$15 \div 3$ means: _____ .

····· Strategy ·····

Division of 0

Division of 0 is always 0.
If there are 0 items, there is
nothing to divide into groups.

Divide.

$0 \div 8 =$ _____

$0 \div 2 =$ _____

$0 \div 7 =$ _____

$0 \div 4 =$ _____

$0 \div 61 =$ _____

$0 \div$ _____ $=$ _____

Division by 0 is not possible. **5 ÷ 0** can't be done.
How could you divide 5 items into 0 groups? It makes no sense.

Division by 1

A number divided by 1
equals the number.

3 dots in 1 group

$3 \div 1 = 3$

6 dots in 1 group

$6 \div 1 = 6$

Divide.

$4 \div 1 =$ _____

$8 \div 1 =$ _____

_____ $\div 1 = 7$

$5 \div 1 =$ _____

$20 \div 1 =$ _____

_____ $\div 1 = 9$

Strategy

A Number Divided by Itself

A number divided by itself equals 1.

4 dots divided into 4 groups is 1 dot in each group.

 →

$4 \div 4 = 1$

Divide.

$9 \div 9 = $ _____ $8 \div 8 = $ _____ $7 \div 7 = $ _____

$15 \div 15 = $ _____ $19 \div 19 = $ _____   _____ $\div 3 = 1$

$6 \div 6 = $ _____ $2 \div 2 = $ _____   _____ $\div 14 = 1$

Review

Match.

$4 \div 1$ • 4 divided into 2 groups

$0 \div 4$ • zero

$4 \div 2$ • four

$4 \div 4$ • one

Strategy

Division by 2

Division by 2 means to divide an amount into two equal sets— to divide the quantity in half.

$8 \div 2 = 4$

Think **Doubles** to divide by 2.

$2 \times ? = 16$

$16 \div 2 = $ _____

$18 \div 2 = $ _____

_____ $\div 2 = 7$

$2 \times ? = 12$

$12 \div 2 = $ _____

$20 \div 2 = $ _____

_____ $\div 2 = 11$

$2 \times ? = 10$

$10 \div 2 = $ _____

$24 \div 2 = $ _____

_____ $\div 2 = 8$

Divide in half.

$44 \div 2 = $ _____

$28 \div 2 = $ _____

$30 \div 2 = $ _____

$32 \div 2 = $ _____

$62 \div 2 = $ _____

$82 \div 2 = $ _____

$50 \div 2 = $ _____

$52 \div 2 = $ _____

$86 \div 2 = $ _____

$66 \div 2 = $ _____

$70 \div 2 = $ _____

$72 \div 2 = $ _____

Strategy

Division by 3

Make three equal groups.

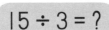

$15 \div 3 = ?$

Imagine you are playing cards with two friends. All three of you need the same number of cards. Deal out 15 cards one at a time.

Three Equal Groups

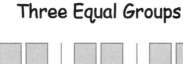

$15 \div 3 = 5$

Divide into three equal groups and solve. Draw dots if it helps you.

$12 \div 3 =$ _____

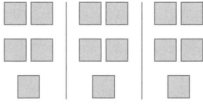

$9 \div 3 =$ _____

$18 \div 3 =$ _____

$21 \div 3 =$ _____

$24 \div 3 =$ _____

$27 \div 3 =$ _____

$30 \div 3 =$ _____

Strategy
Division by 2 and 3

Think multiplication to divide. Solve division problems by thinking of the related multiplication facts.

$18 \div 2 = 9$
$2 \times 9 = 18$

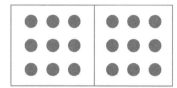

Solve the multiplication fact. Then complete the related division problem.

Multiplication   **Division**

$3 \times 5 = \underline{15}$ ⟷ $\underline{15} \div 3 = 5$

$3 \times 7 = \underline{\hphantom{00}}$ ⟷ $\underline{\hphantom{00}} \div 3 = 7$

$2 \times 12 = \underline{\hphantom{00}}$ ⟷ $\underline{\hphantom{00}} \div 2 = 12$

$2 \times 8 = \underline{\hphantom{00}}$ ⟷ $\underline{\hphantom{00}} \div 2 = 8$

$3 \times 8 = \underline{\hphantom{00}}$ ⟷ $24 \div 3 = \underline{\hphantom{00}}$

$3 \times 9 = \underline{\hphantom{00}}$ ⟷ $\underline{\hphantom{00}} \div 3 = \underline{\hphantom{00}}$

$3 \times 6 = \underline{\hphantom{00}}$ ⟷ $\underline{\hphantom{00}} \div 3 = \underline{\hphantom{00}}$

Strategy

Division by 4

Think multiplication to divide.

A Fact Family

The numbers 3, 4, and 12 make
four related equations:

$3 \times 4 = 12$ $12 \div 3 = 4$
$4 \times 3 = 12$ $12 \div 4 = 3$

Solve. Think about the related multiplication fact.

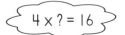

$4 \times ? = 16$

$16 \div 4 =$ _____

$4 \times ? = 20$

$20 \div 4 =$ _____

$4 \times ? = 24$

$24 \div 4 =$ _____

$4 \times ? = 32$

$32 \div 4 =$ _____

$\_ \times \_ = \_$

$12 \div 4 =$ _____

$\_ \times \_ = \_$

$28 \div 4 =$ _____

$\_ \times \_ = \_$

$44 \div 4 =$ _____

$\_ \times \_ = \_$

$48 \div 4 =$ _____

$\_ \times \_ = \_$

$36 \div 4 =$ _____

$\_ \times \_ = \_$

_____ $\div 4 =$ _____

Building Math Fluency • EMC 3036 • © Evan-Moor Corp.

Strategy

Division by 5

Think multiplication to divide.

For each multiplication problem, write the related division equation.
The first one is done for you.

$5 \times 4 = 20 \quad \longleftrightarrow \quad 20 \div 5 = 4$

$5 \times 6 = \boxed{} \quad \longleftrightarrow \quad \boxed{} \div 5 = \underline{}$

$5 \times 7 = \boxed{} \quad \longleftrightarrow \quad \boxed{} \div 5 = \underline{}$

$5 \times 9 = \boxed{} \quad \longleftrightarrow \quad \boxed{} \div 5 = \underline{}$

$5 \times 11 = \boxed{} \quad \longleftrightarrow \quad \boxed{} \div 5 = \underline{}$

$5 \times 12 = \boxed{} \quad \longleftrightarrow \quad \boxed{} \div 5 = \underline{}$

Think **Times 5** to divide by 5.

$25 \div 5 = \underline{} \qquad 40 \div 5 = \underline{} \qquad 35 \div 5 = \underline{}$

$30 \div 5 = \underline{} \qquad 60 \div 5 = \underline{} \qquad 45 \div 5 = \underline{}$

$15 \div 5 = \underline{} \qquad 55 \div 5 = \underline{} \qquad \underline{} \div 5 = 4$

Division by 0, 1, 2, 3, 4

I remember these strategies to help me divide.

- 0 divided by any number is 0.
- A number divided by 1 equals the number.
- A number divided by itself equals 1.
- Think Doubles to divide by 2.
- Think multiplication to divide by 3 and 4.

Divide to solve the problems.

28 ÷ 4 = _____   21 ÷ 3 = _____   18 ÷ 2 = _____

12 ÷ 3 = _____   0 ÷ 6 = _____   21 ÷ 1 = _____

8 ÷ 1 = _____   16 ÷ 2 = _____   20 ÷ 4 = _____

10 ÷ 2 = _____   24 ÷ 24 = _____   0 ÷ 7 = _____

27 ÷ 3 = _____   16 ÷ 4 = _____   9 ÷ 9 = _____

24 ÷ 3 = _____   12 ÷ 4 = _____   15 ÷ 3 = _____

What is your strategy for 48 ÷ 4 = ?

Explain.

_____

_____

_____

Strategy

Division by 6 and 7

Think multiplication to divide.

Fill in the multiplication chart. Use it to solve the division problems.

Multiply	x6	x7
1	6	7
2	12	14
3		
4		
5		
6		
7		
8		
9		
10		
11		
12		

Think **Times 6** to divide by 6.

$18 \div 6 =$ _____ $24 \div 6 =$ _____

$36 \div 6 =$ _____ $48 \div 6 =$ _____

$72 \div 6 =$ _____ $66 \div 6 =$ _____

$30 \div 6 =$ _____ $54 \div 6 =$ _____

Think **Times 7** to divide by 7.

$70 \div 7 =$ _____ $21 \div 7 =$ _____

$63 \div 7 =$ _____ $35 \div 7 =$ _____

$28 \div 7 =$ _____ $77 \div 7 =$ _____

$42 \div 7 =$ _____ $56 \div 7 =$ _____

$49 \div 7 =$ _____ $14 \div 7 =$ _____

$7 \div 7 =$ _____ $84 \div 7 =$ _____

Division by 8, 9, and 12

Name _____

Think multiplication to divide.

Fill in the multiplication chart. Use it to solve the division problems below.

x	1	2	3	4	5	6	7	8	9	10	11	12
8	8	16										
9	9	18										
12	12	24										

Think **Times 8** to divide by 8.

$16 \div 8 = $ _____ $32 \div 8 = $ _____ $48 \div 8 = $ _____

$96 \div 8 = $ _____ $56 \div 8 = $ _____   _____ $\div 8 = 5$

Think **Times 9** to divide by 9.

$36 \div 9 = $ _____ $45 \div 9 = $ _____ $72 \div 9 = $ _____

$63 \div 9 = $ _____ $54 \div 9 = $ _____   _____ $\div 9 = 9$

Think **Times 12** to divide by 12.

$36 \div 12 = $ _____ $48 \div 12 = $ _____ $24 \div 12 = $ _____

$72 \div 12 = $ _____ $60 \div 12 = $ _____   _____ $\div 12 = 12$

     Building Math Fluency • EMC 3036 • © Evan-Moor Corp.

Strategy
Division by 9, 10, and 11

Think multiplication to divide.

Solve the problems. Write letters to match related multiplication and division facts.

b $10 \times 8 =$ 80

___ $9 \times 8 =$ _____

___ $11 \times 7 =$ _____

___ $10 \times 6 =$ _____

___ $9 \times 6 =$ _____

___ $10 \times 12 =$ _____

___ $9 \times 12 =$ _____

___ $11 \times 9 =$ _____

___ $9 \times 9 =$ _____

___ $10 \times 7 =$ _____

___ $9 \times 7 =$ _____

a $72 \div 9 =$ _____

b $80 \div 10 =$ _____

c $54 \div 9 =$ _____

d $60 \div 10 =$ _____

e $77 \div 11 =$ _____

f $120 \div 10 =$ _____

g $81 \div 9 =$ _____

h $108 \div 9 =$ _____

i $99 \div 11 =$ _____

j $63 \div 9 =$ _____

k $70 \div 10 =$ _____

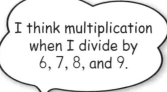

Mixed Strategies Practice

Division by 6, 7, 8, 9

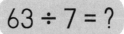

$63 \div 7 = ?$

I think multiplication when I divide by 6, 7, 8, and 9.

7 Times *what* = 63

$7 \times 9 = 63,$

so $63 \div 7 = 9.$

Divide to solve the problems.

$72 \div 9 =$ _____ $36 \div 6 =$ _____ $48 \div 8 =$ _____

$35 \div 7 =$ _____ $64 \div 8 =$ _____ $81 \div 9 =$ _____

$27 \div 9 =$ _____ $49 \div 7 =$ _____ $40 \div 8 =$ _____

$24 \div 6 =$ _____ $36 \div 9 =$ _____ $54 \div 6 =$ _____

$32 \div 8 =$ _____ $21 \div 7 =$ _____ $63 \div 9 =$ _____

$56 \div 7 =$ _____ $42 \div 6 =$ _____ $72 \div 8 =$ _____

What is your strategy for $42 \div 6 = ?$

Explain.

_____

_____

_____

Strategy

Division with Remainders

Think of the nearest multiplication fact.

For **Division with Remainders**, find the multiplication fact that is closest to the dividend but not more than the dividend.

dividend
↓
$11 \div 2 = ?$

I know 2×5 is 10. That's close to 11 but not over 11.
So, I can make two groups of 5 with 1 remaining.

Solve **Division with Remainders**. Think of the nearest multiplication fact.

Problem	My Solution Steps
$13 \div 3 =$ ___4R1___	**What Times 3 is close to 13 (but not more than 13)?** I can divide 13 items into three groups of 4 with 1 remaining. ● ● ● ● | ● ● ● ● | ● ● ● ● | ●
$15 \div 2 =$ _____	**What Times 2 is close to 15?**
$16 \div 5 =$ _____	**What Times 5 is close to 16?**

Strategy

Division with Remainders

Think of the nearest multiplication fact.

Problem	My Solution Steps
$50 \div 7 = ?$	I have 50 items to divide into 7 groups. What Times 7 is close to 50? 6 x 7 is 42. That's not close enough to 50. 8 x 7 is 56. That's over 50. 7 x 7 is 49. That's just one away from 50. I can divide my 50 items into seven groups of 7 and have 1 remaining. $50 \div 7 = 7 \text{ R} 1$
$28 \div 5 = ?$	Explain your solution.
$34 \div 8 = ?$	Explain your solution.

Building Math Fluency • EMC 3036 • © Evan-Moor Corp.

Name _____

Skill Builders ÷3, ÷4, ÷5

Think multiplication to divide.

÷3	÷4	÷5
3 ÷ 3 = _____	4 ÷ 4 = _____	50 ÷ 5 = _____
6 ÷ 3 = _____	8 ÷ 4 = _____	15 ÷ 5 = _____
12 ÷ 3 = _____	16 ÷ 4 = _____	25 ÷ 5 = _____
15 ÷ 3 = _____	20 ÷ 4 = _____	10 ÷ 5 = _____
24 ÷ 3 = _____	32 ÷ 4 = _____	20 ÷ 5 = _____
21 ÷ 3 = _____	48 ÷ 4 = _____	30 ÷ 5 = _____
30 ÷ 3 = _____	40 ÷ 4 = _____	35 ÷ 5 = _____
36 ÷ 3 = _____	28 ÷ 4 = _____	45 ÷ 5 = _____
9 ÷ 3 = _____	12 ÷ 4 = _____	40 ÷ 5 = _____
18 ÷ 3 = _____	24 ÷ 4 = _____	55 ÷ 5 = _____
27 ÷ 3 = _____	36 ÷ 4 = _____	60 ÷ 5 = _____
33 ÷ 3 = _____	44 ÷ 4 = _____	5 ÷ 5 = _____
Record Remainder:	Record Remainder:	Record Remainder:
31 ÷ 3 = _____	22 ÷ 4 = _____	46 ÷ 5 = _____

Name _____

Skill Builders ÷6, ÷7, ÷8

Think multiplication to divide.

÷6	÷7	÷8
12 ÷ 6 = _____	7 ÷ 7 = _____	16 ÷ 8 = _____
24 ÷ 6 = _____	14 ÷ 7 = _____	24 ÷ 8 = _____
48 ÷ 6 = _____	21 ÷ 7 = _____	40 ÷ 8 = _____
18 ÷ 6 = _____	28 ÷ 7 = _____	56 ÷ 8 = _____
36 ÷ 6 = _____	70 ÷ 7 = _____	32 ÷ 8 = _____
42 ÷ 6 = _____	63 ÷ 7 = _____	64 ÷ 8 = _____
30 ÷ 6 = _____	77 ÷ 7 = _____	8 ÷ 8 = _____
54 ÷ 6 = _____	35 ÷ 7 = _____	48 ÷ 8 = _____
60 ÷ 6 = _____	42 ÷ 7 = _____	72 ÷ 8 = _____
66 ÷ 6 = _____	49 ÷ 7 = _____	80 ÷ 8 = _____
72 ÷ 6 = _____	56 ÷ 7 = _____	88 ÷ 8 = _____
6 ÷ 6 = _____	84 ÷ 7 = _____	96 ÷ 8 = _____
Record Remainder:	Record Remainder:	Record Remainder:
61 ÷ 6 = _____	50 ÷ 7 = _____	41 ÷ 8 = _____

Building Math Fluency • EMC 3036 • © Evan-Moor Corp.

Name _____

Skill Builders ÷9, ÷11, ÷12

Think multiplication to divide.

÷9

$9 ÷ 9 =$ _____

$18 ÷ 9 =$ _____

$45 ÷ 9 =$ _____

$90 ÷ 9 =$ _____

$81 ÷ 9 =$ _____

$27 ÷ 9 =$ _____

$36 ÷ 9 =$ _____

$72 ÷ 9 =$ _____

$54 ÷ 9 =$ _____

$63 ÷ 9 =$ _____

$99 ÷ 9 =$ _____

$108 ÷ 9 =$ _____

Record Remainder:

$19 ÷ 9 =$ _____

÷11

$22 ÷ 11 =$ _____

$33 ÷ 11 =$ _____

$55 ÷ 11 =$ _____

$77 ÷ 11 =$ _____

$44 ÷ 11 =$ _____

$88 ÷ 11 =$ _____

$11 ÷ 11 =$ _____

$66 ÷ 11 =$ _____

$99 ÷ 11 =$ _____

$110 ÷ 11 =$ _____

$121 ÷ 11 =$ _____

$132 ÷ 11 =$ _____

Record Remainder:

$25 ÷ 11 =$ _____

÷12

$12 ÷ 12 =$ _____

$24 ÷ 12 =$ _____

$60 ÷ 12 =$ _____

$120 ÷ 12 =$ _____

$108 ÷ 12 =$ _____

$36 ÷ 12 =$ _____

$48 ÷ 12 =$ _____

$96 ÷ 12 =$ _____

$72 ÷ 12 =$ _____

$84 ÷ 12 =$ _____

$132 ÷ 12 =$ _____

$144 ÷ 12 =$ _____

Record Remainder:

$25 ÷ 12 =$ _____

Name _____

Division by Design

Write the quotient below each problem.
Color as directed in the chart below.

18 ÷ 2	6 ÷ 1	60 ÷ 10	16 ÷ 2	12 ÷ 2	54 ÷ 9	54 ÷ 6
18 ÷ 3	99 ÷ 11	14 ÷ 2	70 ÷ 10	21 ÷ 3	81 ÷ 9	12 ÷ 3
66 ÷ 11	63 ÷ 9	27 ÷ 3	48 ÷ 6	63 ÷ 7	28 ÷ 4	48 ÷ 8
32 ÷ 4	14 ÷ 2	64 ÷ 8	25 ÷ 5	56 ÷ 7	77 ÷ 11	24 ÷ 3
24 ÷ 4	56 ÷ 8	9 ÷ 1	80 ÷ 10	36 ÷ 4	35 ÷ 5	8 ÷ 2
40 ÷ 10	18 ÷ 2	49 ÷ 7	7 ÷ 1	42 ÷ 6	72 ÷ 8	42 ÷ 7
90 ÷ 10	30 ÷ 5	44 ÷ 11	40 ÷ 5	36 ÷ 6	16 ÷ 4	45 ÷ 5

Quotient	Color
9	yellow
8	red
7	green
6 or 4	blue
5	your choice

Building Math Fluency • EMC 3036 • © Evan-Moor Corp.

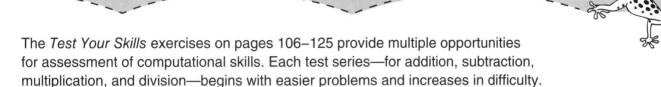

How to Use
Test Your Skills

The *Test Your Skills* exercises on pages 106–125 provide multiple opportunities for assessment of computational skills. Each test series—for addition, subtraction, multiplication, and division—begins with easier problems and increases in difficulty.

Each page in the *Test Your Skills* section can be used multiple times and in different ways to build computational skills and improve fact fluency.

Mixed Strategies Practice

The tests provide the opportunity to practice many of the computational strategies presented in this book. For each problem, students should ask themselves: Which strategy best suits the numbers involved?

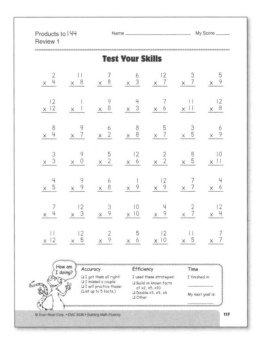

Strategy Focus

Have students select one strategy at a time to practice. They examine the problems and then circle and solve those that fit the focus strategy.

Assessment

Use the tests to determine how students are progressing in their acquisition of number facts. If appropriate, allow students to set their own goals for improvement of computation speed.

Student Self-Evaluation

The record area at the bottom of each *Test Your Skills* page affords students the opportunity to assess their own performance and use of computational strategies. This self-evaluation is an important part of the skill-building process.

After completing a *Test Your Skills* page, allow time for students to share the various strategies they used.

Name _____   My Score _____

Test Your Skills

7 + 4	6 + 5	4 + 3	5 + 5	10 + 1	3 + 9	10 + 0
6 + 3	4 + 5	9 + 2	6 + 6	4 + 1	6 + 2	8 + 1
2 + 2	3 + 5	8 + 3	12 + 0	7 + 5	8 + 4	4 + 2
2 + 7	3 + 3	4 + 6	3 + 8	5 + 2	9 + 3	3 + 4
6 + 4	7 + 3	4 + 4	2 + 8	7 + 2	2 + 0	5 + 3
2 + 5	8 + 2	4 + 0	5 + 4	4 + 8	6 + 6	5 + 7
11 + 1	0 + 8	2 + 9	10 + 2	5 + 6	1 + 9	2 + 7

How am I doing?

Accuracy

❏ I got them all right!
❏ I missed a couple.
❏ I will practice these:
(List up to 5 facts.)

Efficiency

I used these strategies:

❏ Count Up
❏ Doubles
❏ Tens Partners
❏ Other

Time

I finished in:

_____

My next goal is:

_____

Name _____ My Score _____

Test Your Skills

7 + 7	9 + 8	5 + 4	19 + 1	8 + 8	17 + 3	8 + 7
7 + 6	9 + 0	8 + 6	9 + 9	7 + 1	9 + 6	8 + 3
15 + 5	9 + 5	7 + 4	9 + 2	5 + 5	9 + 7	7 + 7
8 + 4	6 + 2	16 + 3	9 + 3	6 + 6	18 + 2	8 + 5
7 + 3	10 + 5	7 + 5	4 + 4	6 + 3	9 + 4	5 + 6
6 + 4	2 + 5	8 + 9	7 + 9	9 + 9	6 + 8	5 + 7
6 + 7	6 + 9	19 + 1	3 + 8	6 + 6	7 + 8	4 + 9

How am I doing?

Accuracy

❏ I got them all right!
❏ I missed a couple.
❏ I will practice these:
(List up to 5 facts.)

Efficiency

I used these strategies:

❏ Count Up
❏ Doubles/Doubles Plus 1 or 2
❏ Tens Partners
❏ Plus 8, 9, 10

Time

I finished in:

_____

My next goal is:

_____

Name _____   My Score _____

Test Your Skills

18 + 2	9 + 4	6 + 6	8 + 5	16 + 3	7 + 5	7 + 7
8 + 6	7 + 3	5 + 5	9 + 8	6 + 2	10 + 5	8 + 3
7 + 4	15 + 5	9 + 0	6 + 5	8 + 7	4 + 4	18 + 2
9 + 2	7 + 6	8 + 4	5 + 4	5 + 2	9 + 3	7 + 8
9 + 5	7 + 1	17 + 3	6 + 3	8 + 8	9 + 7	6 + 9
9 + 9	6 + 4	8 + 3	9 + 6	19 + 1	7 + 7	8 + 6
4 + 4	3 + 6	7 + 9	5 + 6	9 + 8	2 + 9	16 + 4

How am I doing?

Accuracy
❏ I got them all right!
❏ I missed a couple.
❏ I will practice these:
(List up to 5 facts.)

Efficiency
I used these strategies:
❏ Count Up
❏ Doubles/Doubles Plus 1 or 2
❏ Tens Partners
❏ Plus 8, 9, 10

Time
I finished in:
_____

My next goal is:
_____

Name _____   My Score _____

Test Your Skills

15	12	15	11	15	13	11
− 10	− 8	− 9	− 4	− 3	− 6	− 3

12	11	15	13	11	12	15
− 5	− 6	− 8	− 1	− 7	− 3	− 5

12	14	11	14	11	14	13
− 6	− 7	− 2	− 8	− 5	− 6	− 4

11	12	13	13	14	15	14
− 8	− 10	− 5	− 8	− 9	− 7	− 5

12	11	15	15	13	12	13
− 7	− 9	− 0	− 6	− 9	− 4	− 7

15	12	13	14	14	15	12
− 6	− 9	− 8	− 5	− 8	− 3	− 8

12	15	15	12	9	8	15
− 6	− 9	− 5	− 10	− 7	− 6	− 0

How am I doing?

Accuracy

❑ I got them all right!
❑ I missed a couple.
❑ I will practice these:
(List up to 5 facts.)

Efficiency

I used these strategies:
❑ Count Back -1, -2, -3
❑ Count Up from bottom number
❑ Doubles Subtraction
❑ Tens Partners Subtraction

Time

I finished in:

_____

My next goal is:

_____

Name _____   My Score _____

Test Your Skills

13	16	9	17	20	14	17
− 9	− 8	− 5	− 9	− 15	− 7	− 8

11	8	16	14	11	15	13
− 9	− 6	− 1	− 8	− 7	− 9	− 5

20	16	8	14	20	10	15
− 10	− 9	− 3	− 5	− 12	− 6	− 7

9	14	11	18	15	13	10
− 7	− 9	− 6	− 9	− 6	− 8	− 6

12	9	14	16	11	12	15
− 9	− 6	− 6	− 7	− 5	− 7	− 8

12	13	12	19	12	13	19
− 3	− 6	− 8	− 7	− 6	− 7	− 5

11	18	20	9	16	15	11
− 8	− 8	− 4	− 4	− 7	− 6	− 9

How am I doing?

Accuracy
❏ I got them all right!
❏ I missed a couple.
❏ I will practice these:
(List up to 5 facts.)

Efficiency
I used these strategies:
❏ Count Back -1, -2, -3
❏ Count Up from bottom number
❏ Doubles Subtraction
❏ Minus 10, 9, 8

Time
I finished in:
_____

My next goal is:
_____

Name _____   My Score _____

Test Your Skills

20	9	12	13	11	14	16
− 10	− 5	− 7	− 5	− 9	− 7	− 0

14	11	16	15	16	13	20
− 5	− 5	− 1	− 6	− 7	− 8	− 8

10	16	8	12	17	15	19
− 6	− 9	− 3	− 9	− 9	− 8	− 5

13	20	12	14	18	11	20
− 6	− 15	− 6	− 8	− 9	− 6	− 7

15	14	13	9	16	12	13
− 7	− 6	− 9	− 6	− 8	− 8	− 6

11	9	15	17	13	14	16
− 7	− 7	− 9	− 8	− 7	− 9	− 9

14	10	20	11	8	19	18
− 5	− 7	− 4	− 8	− 6	− 7	− 8

How am I doing?

Accuracy
❑ I got them all right!
❑ I missed a couple.
❑ I will practice these:
(List up to 5 facts.)

Efficiency
I used these strategies:
❑ Count Back -1, -2, -3
❑ Count Up from bottom number
❑ Doubles Subtraction
❑ Minus 10, 9, 8

Time
I finished in:

_____

My next goal is:

_____

Name _____   My Score _____

Test Your Skills

```
    5          3          5          6          8          7          4
  x 2        x 4        x 5        x 0        x 1        x 2        x 4


    3         10          2          4          8          5          6
  x 8        x 2        x 3        x 2        x 2        x 4        x 3


    9          6          8         12          4          2          3
  x 2        x 3        x 3        x 2        x 5        x 8        x 5


    2          7          2         11          4          6          2
  x 6        x 3        x 9        x 1        x 3        x 4        x 5


    3          2         10          5          4          3         11
  x 0        x 4        x 1        x 3        x 6        x 7        x 2


    6          6          1          2          9          3          3
  x 4        x 2        x 7        x 2        x 0        x 3        x 7


    3          8          2          3         12          4          1
  x 2        x 3        x 7        x 6        x 1        x 6        x 2
```

How am I doing?

Accuracy
❏ I got them all right!
❏ I missed a couple.
❏ I will practice these:
(List up to 5 facts.)

Efficiency
I used these strategies:
❏ Times 1
❏ Doubles Facts
❏ Doubles Times 2
❏ Skip Count

Time
I finished in:
_____

My next goal is:
_____

Name _____   My Score _____

Test Your Skills

```
  4        6        4        2        3        4       12
x 2      x 3      x 5      x 9      x 8      x 3      x 2
```

```
  3       11        4        3       12        4        3
x 5      x 2      x 4      x 6      x 1      x 6      x 3
```

```
  8        4        5        2        6        3        7
x 2      x 6      x 4      x 5      x 2      x 4      x 3
```

```
  1        6        9       10        2        9        1
x 7      x 0      x 2      x 1      x 3      x 0      x 2
```

```
 11        7        3        5        6        3        8
x 1      x 2      x 6      x 2      x 4      x 0      x 3
```

```
  5        3       10        2        2        8        6
x 3      x 7      x 2      x 4      x 7      x 1      x 4
```

```
  5        3        3        2        2        8        2
x 5      x 2      x 7      x 8      x 2      x 3      x 6
```

How am I doing?

Accuracy
❏ I got them all right!
❏ I missed a couple.
❏ I will practice these:
(List up to 5 facts.)

Efficiency
I used these strategies:
❏ Times 1
❏ Doubles Facts
❏ Doubles Times 2
❏ Skip Count

Time
I finished in:
_____
My next goal is:
_____

Name _____   My Score _____

Test Your Skills

6 x 7	8 x 4	7 x 9	5 x 6	12 x 4	9 x 3	8 x 7
7 x 9	12 x 6	11 x 6	9 x 9	10 x 5	11 x 4	7 x 5
6 x 9	12 x 3	4 x 7	10 x 7	5 x 9	7 x 7	8 x 9
8 x 6	11 x 7	6 x 6	9 x 8	9 x 7	12 x 5	3 x 9
6 x 5	8 x 8	7 x 8	11 x 3	9 x 4	8 x 5	11 x 5
7 x 7	4 x 8	9 x 7	7 x 4	8 x 9	9 x 5	12 x 6
4 x 9	7 x 6	12 x 3	5 x 8	9 x 6	5 x 7	6 x 8

How am I doing?

Accuracy
❏ I got them all right!
❏ I missed a couple.
❏ I will practice these:
(List up to 5 facts.)

Efficiency
I used these strategies:
❏ Build on known facts
   of x2, x5, x10
❏ Double x3, x4, x6
❏ Other

Time
I finished in:

_____

My next goal is:

_____

Name _____   My Score _____

Test Your Skills

4 × 9	11 × 6	7 × 8	6 × 6	5 × 8	9 × 8	7 × 4
7 × 9	8 × 6	5 × 6	10 × 5	5 × 9	11 × 4	4 × 8
7 × 7	8 × 4	3 × 9	12 × 3	8 × 8	7 × 9	9 × 6
12 × 5	7 × 8	9 × 9	5 × 7	12 × 4	7 × 6	8 × 5
4 × 7	9 × 5	11 × 7	6 × 5	8 × 7	12 × 6	7 × 9
11 × 3	7 × 5	9 × 7	12 × 3	6 × 8	9 × 4	6 × 9
10 × 7	9 × 3	12 × 4	12 × 6	11 × 5	8 × 9	6 × 7

How am I doing?

Accuracy
❏ I got them all right!
❏ I missed a couple.
❏ I will practice these:
(List up to 5 facts.)

Efficiency
I used these strategies:
❏ Build on known facts
of x2, x5, x10
❏ Double x3, x4, x6
❏ Other

Time
I finished in:

_____

My next goal is:

_____

Name _____   My Score _____

Test Your Skills

12 × 12	12 × 7	10 × 11	12 × 9	10 × 9	12 × 10	11 × 11
11 × 10	10 × 9	12 × 12	12 × 11	12 × 7	12 × 9	10 × 11
12 × 11	12 × 7	11 × 12	10 × 12	12 × 8	11 × 8	12 × 10
12 × 8	10 × 10	11 × 9	10 × 11	12 × 9	12 × 12	11 × 11
12 × 12	11 × 12	10 × 12	10 × 9	12 × 8	12 × 10	10 × 10
12 × 11	11 × 10	12 × 9	10 × 10	11 × 9	12 × 8	12 × 7
12 × 10	11 × 11	11 × 8	11 × 12	10 × 11	12 × 7	12 × 9

How am I doing?

Accuracy
❑ I got them all right!
❑ I missed a couple.
❑ I will practice these:
(List up to 5 facts.)

Efficiency
I used these strategies:
❑ Build on known facts
  of x2, x5, x10
❑ Double x3, x4, x6
❑ Other

Time
I finished in:

_____

My next goal is:

_____

Building Math Fluency • EMC 3036 • © Evan-Moor Corp.

Name _____ My Score _____

Test Your Skills

2 x 4	11 x 8	7 x 8	6 x 3	12 x 7	3 x 7	5 x 9
12 x 12	1 x 1	9 x 8	4 x 3	7 x 6	11 x 11	12 x 8
8 x 4	9 x 7	6 x 2	8 x 8	5 x 7	3 x 5	6 x 9
3 x 3	9 x 0	5 x 2	12 x 6	2 x 2	8 x 5	10 x 11
4 x 5	9 x 9	6 x 8	1 x 9	12 x 9	7 x 7	4 x 6
7 x 4	12 x 3	3 x 9	10 x 10	4 x 9	2 x 7	12 x 4
11 x 12	12 x 5	2 x 9	5 x 6	12 x 10	11 x 5	7 x 7

How am I doing?

Accuracy

❏ I got them all right!
❏ I missed a couple.
❏ I will practice these:
(List up to 5 facts.)

Efficiency

I used these strategies:
❏ Build on known facts
of x2, x5, x10
❏ Double x3, x4, x6
❏ Other

Time

I finished in:

_____

My next goal is:

_____

Name _____   My Score _____

Test Your Skills

2 × 3	4 × 4	3 × 3	4 × 1	12 × 2	9 × 4	2 × 8
6 × 5	8 × 8	3 × 4	12 × 8	2 × 5	12 × 4	8 × 7
7 × 9	4 × 2	11 × 1	7 × 5	9 × 3	10 × 9	5 × 4
10 × 12	12 × 5	1 × 8	11 × 11	8 × 6	9 × 9	3 × 8
7 × 2	8 × 9	5 × 3	12 × 9	3 × 2	9 × 5	12 × 4
2 × 6	12 × 11	6 × 4	4 × 8	12 × 7	7 × 3	9 × 2
4 × 7	5 × 8	7 × 7	3 × 6	6 × 7	5 × 5	9 × 6

How am I doing?

Accuracy
❏ I got them all right!
❏ I missed a couple.
❏ I will practice these:
(List up to 5 facts.)

Efficiency
I used these strategies:
❏ Build on known facts
   of x2, x5, x10
❏ Double x3, x4, x6
❏ Other

Time
I finished in:
_____

My next goal is:
_____

Name _____   My Score _____

Test Your Skills

21 ÷ 7 = _____   24 ÷ 4 = _____   25 ÷ 5 = _____

10 ÷ 5 = _____   0 ÷ 7 = _____   3 ÷ 3 = _____

12 ÷ 2 = _____   24 ÷ 6 = _____   20 ÷ 4 = _____

12 ÷ 12 = _____   18 ÷ 9 = _____   20 ÷ 2 = _____

24 ÷ 3 = _____   14 ÷ 2 = _____   12 ÷ 1 = _____

24 ÷ 12 = _____   12 ÷ 4 = _____   12 ÷ 3 = _____

20 ÷ 5 = _____   24 ÷ 8 = _____   12 ÷ 6 = _____

8 ÷ 4 = _____   6 ÷ 3 = _____   9 ÷ 3 = _____

18 ÷ 3 = _____   11 ÷ 1 = _____   24 ÷ 2 = _____

16 ÷ 2 = _____   22 ÷ 2 = _____   18 ÷ 6 = _____

22 ÷ 11 = _____   16 ÷ 8 = _____   12 ÷ 1 = _____

24 ÷ 3 = _____   15 ÷ 5 = _____   16 ÷ 4 = _____

15 ÷ 3 = _____   14 ÷ 7 = _____   21 ÷ 3 = _____

20 ÷ 10 = _____   11 ÷ 11 = _____   18 ÷ 2 = _____

How am I doing?

Accuracy
❏ I got them all right!
❏ I missed a couple.
❏ I will practice these:
(List up to 5 facts.)

Efficiency
I used these strategies:
❏ Divide by 1
❏ Divide by Self
❏ Doubles Facts
❏ Think Multiplication

Time
I finished in:
_____
My next goal is:
_____

Name _____   My Score _____

Test Your Skills

$11 \div 1 =$ _____ $15 \div 5 =$ _____ $22 \div 2 =$ _____

$15 \div 3 =$ _____ $22 \div 11 =$ _____ $20 \div 10 =$ _____

$24 \div 6 =$ _____ $24 \div 8 =$ _____ $12 \div 4 =$ _____

$14 \div 7 =$ _____ $16 \div 8 =$ _____ $11 \div 11 =$ _____

$24 \div 2 =$ _____ $16 \div 4 =$ _____ $18 \div 6 =$ _____

$20 \div 2 =$ _____ $25 \div 5 =$ _____ $12 \div 1 =$ _____

$12 \div 3 =$ _____ $12 \div 6 =$ _____ $20 \div 4 =$ _____

$21 \div 3 =$ _____ $12 \div 1 =$ _____ $18 \div 2 =$ _____

$18 \div 9 =$ _____ $24 \div 4 =$ _____ $24 \div 3 =$ _____

$18 \div 3 =$ _____ $14 \div 2 =$ _____ $16 \div 2 =$ _____

$12 \div 2 =$ _____ $20 \div 5 =$ _____ $24 \div 12 =$ _____

$12 \div 12 =$ _____ $24 \div 3 =$ _____ $21 \div 7 =$ _____

$8 \div 2 =$ _____ $0 \div 9 =$ _____ $10 \div 2 =$ _____

$6 \div 2 =$ _____ $9 \div 3 =$ _____ $5 \div 5 =$ _____

How am I doing?

Accuracy
❏ I got them all right!
❏ I missed a couple.
❏ I will practice these:
(List up to 5 facts.)

Efficiency
I used these strategies:
❏ Divide by 1
❏ Divide by Self
❏ Doubles Facts
❏ Think Multiplication

Time
I finished in:

_____

My next goal is:

_____

Name _____   My Score _____

Test Your Skills

$45 ÷ 5 =$ _____ $40 ÷ 5 =$ _____ $35 ÷ 7 =$ _____

$56 ÷ 7 =$ _____ $80 ÷ 10 =$ _____ $44 ÷ 4 =$ _____

$36 ÷ 6 =$ _____ $30 ÷ 6 =$ _____ $72 ÷ 6 =$ _____

$72 ÷ 12 =$ _____ $63 ÷ 9 =$ _____ $48 ÷ 8 =$ _____

$33 ÷ 11 =$ _____ $32 ÷ 8 =$ _____ $72 ÷ 8 =$ _____

$70 ÷ 7 =$ _____ $54 ÷ 9 =$ _____ $33 ÷ 3 =$ _____

$50 ÷ 5 =$ _____ $42 ÷ 6 =$ _____ $77 ÷ 7 =$ _____

$66 ÷ 11 =$ _____ $63 ÷ 7 =$ _____ $27 ÷ 3 =$ _____

$28 ÷ 4 =$ _____ $54 ÷ 6 =$ _____ $60 ÷ 5 =$ _____

$56 ÷ 8 =$ _____ $40 ÷ 4 =$ _____ $32 ÷ 4 =$ _____

$30 ÷ 5 =$ _____ $27 ÷ 9 =$ _____ $60 ÷ 12 =$ _____

$60 ÷ 10 =$ _____ $44 ÷ 11 =$ _____ $63 ÷ 9 =$ _____

$28 ÷ 7 =$ _____ $30 ÷ 6 =$ _____ $54 ÷ 6 =$ _____

$80 ÷ 10 =$ _____ $77 ÷ 11 =$ _____ $81 ÷ 9 =$ _____

How am I doing?

Accuracy
❏ I got them all right!
❏ I missed a couple.
❏ I will practice these:
(List up to 5 facts.)

Efficiency
I used these strategies:
❏ Think Multiplication
❏ Other:

Time
I finished in:

_____

My next goal is:

_____

Name _____   My Score _____

Test Your Skills

36 ÷ 3 = _____   36 ÷ 4 = _____   50 ÷ 10 = _____

66 ÷ 6 = _____   60 ÷ 6 = _____   56 ÷ 8 = _____

44 ÷ 11 = _____   48 ÷ 12 = _____   45 ÷ 9 = _____

64 ÷ 8 = _____   84 ÷ 12 = _____   81 ÷ 9 = _____

30 ÷ 10 = _____   40 ÷ 10 = _____   42 ÷ 7 = _____

63 ÷ 9 = _____   55 ÷ 5 = _____   54 ÷ 6 = _____

48 ÷ 6 = _____   49 ÷ 7 = _____   48 ÷ 4 = _____

60 ÷ 5 = _____   70 ÷ 10 = _____   72 ÷ 9 = _____

36 ÷ 12 = _____   30 ÷ 3 = _____   42 ÷ 6 = _____

55 ÷ 11 = _____   63 ÷ 7 = _____   40 ÷ 4 = _____

35 ÷ 7 = _____   40 ÷ 8 = _____   54 ÷ 9 = _____

81 ÷ 9 = _____   72 ÷ 8 = _____   27 ÷ 9 = _____

35 ÷ 5 = _____   36 ÷ 9 = _____   28 ÷ 4 = _____

80 ÷ 8 = _____   72 ÷ 6 = _____   48 ÷ 8 = _____

How am I doing?

Accuracy
❏ I got them all right!
❏ I missed a couple.
❏ I will practice these:
(List up to 5 facts.)

Efficiency
I used these strategies:
❏ Think Multiplication
❏ Other:

Time
I finished in:
_____

My next goal is:
_____

Name _____   My Score _____

Test Your Skills

84 ÷ 7 = _____   108 ÷ 12 = _____   96 ÷ 8 = _____

144 ÷ 12 = _____   120 ÷ 10 = _____   110 ÷ 10 = _____

108 ÷ 9 = _____   84 ÷ 12 = _____   96 ÷ 12 = _____

132 ÷ 12 = _____   99 ÷ 9 = _____   132 ÷ 11 = _____

84 ÷ 12 = _____   99 ÷ 11 = _____   121 ÷ 11 = _____

90 ÷ 9 = _____   88 ÷ 8 = _____   84 ÷ 7 = _____

108 ÷ 12 = _____   96 ÷ 12 = _____   108 ÷ 9 = _____

84 ÷ 7 = _____   132 ÷ 11 = _____   144 ÷ 12 = _____

88 ÷ 11 = _____   110 ÷ 10 = _____   99 ÷ 9 = _____

90 ÷ 10 = _____   84 ÷ 7 = _____   132 ÷ 11 = _____

132 ÷ 12 = _____   88 ÷ 8 = _____   110 ÷ 11 = _____

120 ÷ 12 = _____   108 ÷ 12 = _____   120 ÷ 10 = _____

99 ÷ 9 = _____   100 ÷ 10 = _____   96 ÷ 8 = _____

84 ÷ 7 = _____   110 ÷ 11 = _____   84 ÷ 12 = _____

How am I doing?

Accuracy
❑ I got them all right!
❑ I missed a couple.
❑ I will practice these:
(List up to 5 facts.)

Efficiency
I used these strategies:
❑ Think Multiplication
❑ Other:

Time
I finished in:
_____
My next goal is:
_____

Name _____   My Score _____

Test Your Skills

$27 ÷ 9 =$ _____ $54 ÷ 9 =$ _____ $72 ÷ 9 =$ _____

$60 ÷ 12 =$ _____ $144 ÷ 12 =$ _____ $40 ÷ 8 =$ _____

$64 ÷ 8 =$ _____ $132 ÷ 12 =$ _____ $96 ÷ 12 =$ _____

$18 ÷ 6 =$ _____ $108 ÷ 9 =$ _____ $132 ÷ 11 =$ _____

$90 ÷ 10 =$ _____ $72 ÷ 12 =$ _____ $81 ÷ 9 =$ _____

$30 ÷ 6 =$ _____ $21 ÷ 7 =$ _____ $28 ÷ 7 =$ _____

$88 ÷ 11 =$ _____ $20 ÷ 5 =$ _____ $49 ÷ 7 =$ _____

$12 ÷ 4 =$ _____ $84 ÷ 12 =$ _____ $110 ÷ 10 =$ _____

$24 ÷ 8 =$ _____ $63 ÷ 9 =$ _____ $24 ÷ 6 =$ _____

$42 ÷ 7 =$ _____ $48 ÷ 8 =$ _____ $32 ÷ 8 =$ _____

$36 ÷ 9 =$ _____ $99 ÷ 11 =$ _____ $108 ÷ 12 =$ _____

$100 ÷ 10 =$ _____ $36 ÷ 9 =$ _____ $15 ÷ 5 =$ _____

$8 ÷ 2 =$ _____ $55 ÷ 5 =$ _____ $9 ÷ 3 =$ _____

$45 ÷ 5 =$ _____ $12 ÷ 6 =$ _____ $35 ÷ 7 =$ _____

How am I doing?

Accuracy
❏ I got them all right!
❏ I missed a couple.
❏ I will practice these:
(List up to 5 facts.)

Efficiency
I used these strategies:
❏ Think Multiplication
❏ Other:

Time
I finished in:

_____

My next goal is:

_____

Name _____   My Score _____

Test Your Skills

$27 \div 3 =$ _____ $54 \div 6 =$ _____ $72 \div 8 =$ _____

$60 \div 5 =$ _____ $144 \div 12 =$ _____ $64 \div 8 =$ _____

$18 \div 3 =$ _____ $132 \div 11 =$ _____ $49 \div 7 =$ _____

$90 \div 9 =$ _____ $108 \div 12 =$ _____ $40 \div 5 =$ _____

$30 \div 5 =$ _____ $72 \div 6 =$ _____ $96 \div 8 =$ _____

$88 \div 8 =$ _____ $21 \div 3 =$ _____ $132 \div 12 =$ _____

$48 \div 4 =$ _____ $20 \div 4 =$ _____ $81 \div 9 =$ _____

$24 \div 3 =$ _____ $84 \div 7 =$ _____ $28 \div 4 =$ _____

$42 \div 6 =$ _____ $63 \div 7 =$ _____ $108 \div 12 =$ _____

$36 \div 4 =$ _____ $48 \div 6 =$ _____ $24 \div 4 =$ _____

$100 \div 10 =$ _____ $99 \div 9 =$ _____ $36 \div 6 =$ _____

$8 \div 4 =$ _____ $36 \div 4 =$ _____ $32 \div 4 =$ _____

$45 \div 9 =$ _____ $55 \div 11 =$ _____ $108 \div 9 =$ _____

$25 \div 5 =$ _____ $56 \div 7 =$ _____ $15 \div 3 =$ _____

How am
I doing?

Accuracy
❏ I got them all right!
❏ I missed a couple.
❏ I will practice these:
(List up to 5 facts.)

Efficiency
I used these strategies:
❏ Think Multiplication
❏ Other:

Time
I finished in:
_____

My next goal is:
_____

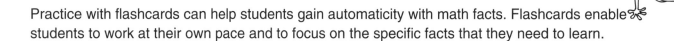

How to Use
Facts Flashcards

Practice with flashcards can help students gain automaticity with math facts. Flashcards enable students to work at their own pace and to focus on the specific facts that they need to learn.

Prepare the Flashcards

- Reproduce the cards that students need to practice. Within each operation, the cards progress from easier to more difficult facts. Keep the cards to a manageable number; add new cards as facts are mastered.

- Students cut the cards apart and write the answers on the backs of the cards. Be sure to check the answers so that students do not practice the wrong answers.

- Have students store the cards in an envelope or self-sealing plastic bag.

- Use the template on page 145 if you wish to create flashcards for a specific strategy or for individual needs.

Tips for Practicing the Flashcards

- When students practice independently, encourage them to softly say the facts aloud so they both see and hear them.

- Have students practice with a partner. This is more fun and it ensures that students are computing each answer and not just looking at the answer. If an answer is incorrect, the partner should say, for example, "No, $8 + 6$ is 14." Then the answering student should repeat the equation aloud.

- Have students sort and then practice the cards by the strategies they would use to compute the answers. Cards can be categorized into piles of:

Addition & Subtraction	Multiplication & Division
Easy facts—Plus 1, Minus 0, Count Up	Easy Facts—Times 1, Divide by 0 or 1
Doubles	Doubles
Tens Partners	Triples
Plus or Minus 9 or 10	Think Times Ten
Hidden Doubles	Square Numbers
Fact Families	Fact Families

- Allow students to personalize their cards to show the strategies used to compute the answers.

Hidden Doubles

$6 + 6 + 1$

$6 + 7$

Double 6 and add 1

$12 + 1 = 13$

Addition

Think Times 10

9×9

That's $(9 \times 10) - 9$

$90 - 9 = 81$

Multiplication

Tips for Flashcards Study

Flashcards provide a unique way to build fact power. You will find that even the first step of preparing your flashcards, which is to write the answers on card backs, helps improve fact mastery. Here are tips to make flashcards study work for you.

Sort your cards into groups

This lets you focus on learning one group of cards at a time. There are several ways to organize your cards. Over time, try to make all the different categories.

Sort cards by type:

- Doubles facts

Doubles Facts	Doubles Facts
2 x 9	6 x 2
Multiplication	Multiplication

- Square numbers

Square Numbers	Square Numbers
8 x 8	49 ÷ 7
Multiplication	Division

Put fact families together:

3 x 6 / 6 x 3	18 ÷ 3	18 ÷ 6
Multiplication	Division	Division

Group cards into two piles:

- Facts I Know Well
- Facts I Need to Learn

Practice with a partner

- Have your partner show you one of your facts cards.
- Tell your partner the answer.
- Your partner should say, "Yes (or no), the answer is ____."

Target your learning strengths

- Say the facts out loud.
- Trace the facts with your finger.
- Add words or pictures to your cards.

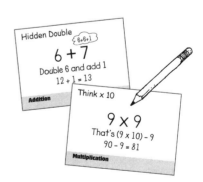

Other ways to study with flashcards:

_____

_____

5 + 5	10 + 0	9 + 1	8 + 2
Addition	Addition	Addition	Addition
7 + 3	6 + 4	8 + 3	7 + 4
Addition	Addition	Addition	Addition
9 + 3	8 + 4	6 + 5	7 + 5
Addition	Addition	Addition	Addition
6 + 6	7 + 6	7 + 7	8 + 8
Addition	Addition	Addition	Addition

9 + 6	12 + 4	8 + 6	11 + 3
Addition	Addition	Addition	Addition
9 + 7	9 + 5	8 + 7	8 + 5
Addition	Addition	Addition	Addition
9 + 9	15 + 5	9 + 8	11 + 5
Addition	Addition	Addition	Addition
9 + 4	13 + 7	10 + 9	12 + 6
Addition	Addition	Addition	Addition

$12 - 6$	$10 - 9$	$11 - 8$	$10 - 5$
Subtraction	Subtraction	Subtraction	Subtraction
$12 - 8$	$10 - 6$	$11 - 7$	$10 - 7$
Subtraction	Subtraction	Subtraction	Subtraction
$13 - 5$	$11 - 6$	$12 - 7$	$10 - 4$
Subtraction	Subtraction	Subtraction	Subtraction
$16 - 8$	$14 - 7$	$13 - 6$	$11 - 5$
Subtraction	Subtraction	Subtraction	Subtraction

16 – 7	14 – 6	16 – 9	14 – 8
Subtraction	Subtraction	Subtraction	Subtraction
17 – 9	14 – 9	17 – 8	14 – 5
Subtraction	Subtraction	Subtraction	Subtraction
13 – 7	15 – 7	18 – 9	15 – 6
Subtraction	Subtraction	Subtraction	Subtraction
13 – 9	15 – 9	13 – 8	15 – 8
Subtraction	Subtraction	Subtraction	Subtraction

Multiplication

3×2
2×3

2×2

0×7
7×0

1×9
9×1

4×4

4×3
3×4

4×2
2×4

3×3

5×4
4×5

5×3
3×5

5×2
2×5

5×1
1×5

6×6

6×3
3×6

6×2
2×6

5×5

Multiplication

Building Math Fluency • EMC 3036 • © Evan-Moor Corp.

Multiplication flashcards

6 × 4 / 4 × 6	6 × 5 / 5 × 6	7 × 2 / 2 × 7
Multiplication	Multiplication	Multiplication
7 × 3 / 3 × 7	7 × 4 / 4 × 7	7 × 7
Multiplication	Multiplication	Multiplication
8 × 2 / 2 × 8	8 × 3 / 3 × 8	7 × 6 / 6 × 7
Multiplication	Multiplication	Multiplication
8 × 6 / 6 × 8	8 × 7 / 7 × 8	7 × 5 / 5 × 7
Multiplication	Multiplication	Multiplication
		8 × 5 / 5 × 8
		Multiplication
		8 × 4 / 4 × 8
		Multiplication
		9 × 2 / 2 × 9
		Multiplication
		8 × 8
		Multiplication

9×3 3×9	9×4 4×9	9×5 5×9	9×6 6×9

9×7 7×9	9×8 8×9	9×9	1×10 10×1

2×10 10×2	3×10 10×3	4×10 10×4	5×10 10×5

6×10 10×6	7×10 10×7	8×10 10×8	10×9 9×10

Multiplication

11×4
4×11
Multiplication

11×8
8×11
Multiplication

11×12
12×11
Multiplication

12×4
4×12
Multiplication

11×3
3×11
Multiplication

11×7
7×11
Multiplication

11×11
Multiplication

12×3
3×12
Multiplication

11×2
2×11
Multiplication

11×6
6×11
Multiplication

11×10
10×11
Multiplication

12×2
2×12
Multiplication

11×1
1×11
Multiplication

11×5
5×11
Multiplication

11×9
9×11
Multiplication

12×1
1×12
Multiplication

12×5 5×12	12×6 6×12	12×7 7×12	12×8 8×12
Multiplication	**Multiplication**	**Multiplication**	**Multiplication**
12×9 9×12	12×10 10×12	12×11 11×12	11×12 12×11
Multiplication	**Multiplication**	**Multiplication**	**Multiplication**

$0 \div 3$	$4 \div 2$	$7 \div 7$	$0 \div 9$
Division	Division	Division	Division
$6 \div 3$	$6 \div 2$	$5 \div 5$	$5 \div 1$
Division	Division	Division	Division
$10 \div 2$	$9 \div 3$	$8 \div 2$	$8 \div 4$
Division	Division	Division	Division
$12 \div 4$	$12 \div 3$	$12 \div 2$	$10 \div 5$
Division	Division	Division	Division

$15 \div 3$	$14 \div 7$	$14 \div 2$	$12 \div 6$
Division	**Division**	**Division**	**Division**
$18 \div 9$	$16 \div 2$	$16 \div 8$	$15 \div 5$
Division	**Division**	**Division**	**Division**
$20 \div 4$	$18 \div 6$	$18 \div 3$	$18 \div 2$
Division	**Division**	**Division**	**Division**
$21 \div 7$	$20 \div 10$	$20 \div 2$	$20 \div 5$
Division	**Division**	**Division**	**Division**

$21 \div 3$	$24 \div 6$	$24 \div 4$	$24 \div 8$
Division	Division	Division	Division
$24 \div 3$	$25 \div 5$	$27 \div 3$	$27 \div 9$
Division	Division	Division	Division
$28 \div 4$	$28 \div 7$	$30 \div 10$	$30 \div 3$
Division	Division	Division	Division
$30 \div 5$	$30 \div 6$	$32 \div 8$	$32 \div 4$
Division	Division	Division	Division

35 ÷ 7	Division	35 ÷ 5	Division	36 ÷ 4	Division	36 ÷ 9	Division
40 ÷ 10	Division	40 ÷ 4	Division	40 ÷ 5	Division	40 ÷ 8	Division
42 ÷ 6	Division	42 ÷ 7	Division	45 ÷ 5	Division	45 ÷ 9	Division
48 ÷ 8	Division	48 ÷ 6	Division	49 ÷ 7	Division	50 ÷ 5	Division

$63 \div 7$	$70 \div 10$	$80 \div 8$	$100 \div 10$
Division	Division	Division	Division
$54 \div 9$	$70 \div 7$	$81 \div 9$	$90 \div 10$
Division	Division	Division	Division
$54 \div 6$	$64 \div 8$	$72 \div 9$	$90 \div 9$
Division	Division	Division	Division
$50 \div 10$	$63 \div 9$	$72 \div 8$	$80 \div 10$
Division	Division	Division	Division

$22 \div 11$

$44 \div 11$

$66 \div 11$

$88 \div 11$

$22 \div 2$

$44 \div 4$

$66 \div 6$

$88 \div 8$

$11 \div 11$

$33 \div 11$

$55 \div 11$

$77 \div 11$

$11 \div 1$

$33 \div 3$

$55 \div 5$

$77 \div 7$

Division	Division	Division	Division
$110 \div 11$	$12 \div 1$	$36 \div 3$	$100 \div 10$
$110 \div 10$	$132 \div 12$	$24 \div 12$	$48 \div 12$
$99 \div 11$	$132 \div 11$	$24 \div 2$	$48 \div 4$
$99 \div 9$	$121 \div 11$	$12 \div 12$	$36 \div 12$

$72 \div 12$	$72 \div 6$	$60 \div 12$	$60 \div 5$
Division	**Division**	**Division**	**Division**
$96 \div 12$	$96 \div 8$	$84 \div 12$	$84 \div 7$
Division	**Division**	**Division**	**Division**
$120 \div 12$	$120 \div 10$	$108 \div 12$	$108 \div 9$
Division	**Division**	**Division**	**Division**
			$144 \div 12$
Division	**Division**	**Division**	**Division**

Strategy:

Strategy:

Strategy:

Strategy:

Strategy:

Strategy:

Strategy:

Strategy:

Strategy:

Strategy:

Strategy:

Strategy:

Answer Key

Page 11

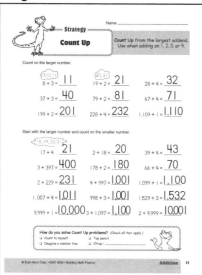

Strategy — Count Up
Count Up from the largest addend. Use when adding on 1, 2, 3, or 4.

Count on the larger number.

8 + 3 = 11   19 + 2 = 21   28 + 4 = 32
37 + 3 = 40   79 + 2 = 81   67 + 4 = 71
199 + 2 = 201   228 + 4 = 232   1,109 + 1 = 1,110

Start with the larger number and count on the smaller number.

17 + 4 = 21   2 + 18 = 20   39 + 4 = 43
3 + 397 = 400   178 + 2 = 180   66 + 4 = 70
2 + 229 = 231   4 + 997 = 1,001   1,099 + 1 = 1,100
1,007 + 4 = 1,011   998 + 3 = 1,001   1,529 + 3 = 1,532
9,999 + 1 = 10,000   3 + 1,097 = 1,100   2 + 9,999 = 10,001

How do you solve Count Up problems? (Check all that apply.)
☐ Count to myself   ☐ Tap pencil
☐ Imagine a number line   ☐ Other

Page 12

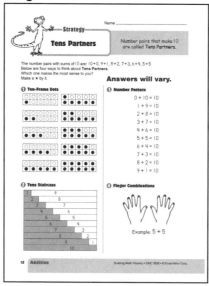

Strategy — Tens Partners
Number pairs that make 10 are called Tens Partners.

The number pairs with sums of 10 are: 10+0, 9+1, 8+2, 7+3, 6+4, 5+5
Below are four ways to think about Tens Partners.
Which one makes the most sense to you?
Make a ★ by it.

Answers will vary.

① Ten-Frame Dots

③ Number Pattern
0 + 10 = 10
1 + 9 = 10
2 + 8 = 10
3 + 7 = 10
4 + 6 = 10
5 + 5 = 10
6 + 4 = 10
7 + 3 = 10
8 + 2 = 10
9 + 1 = 10

② Tens Staircase

④ Finger Combinations

Example: 5 + 5

Page 13

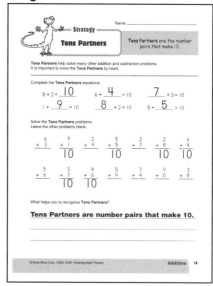

Strategy — Tens Partners
Tens Partners are the number pairs that make 10.

Tens Partners help solve many other addition and subtraction problems. It is important to know the Tens Partners by heart.

Complete the Tens Partners equations.

8 + 2 = 10   6 + 4 = 10   7 + 3 = 10
1 + 9 = 10   8 + 2 = 10   5 + 5 = 10

Solve the Tens Partners problems.
Leave the other problems blank.

6	9	2	5	2	6
+3	+1	+9	+5	+8	+4
10	10	10	10	10	10

5	3	4	5	9	3
+6	+1	+4	+7	+0	+1
10	10				

What helps you to recognize Tens Partners?

Tens Partners are number pairs that make 10.

Page 14

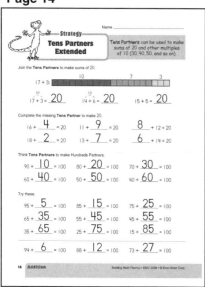

Strategy — Tens Partners Extended
Tens Partners can be used to make sums of 20 and other multiples of 10 (30, 40, 50, and so on).

Join the Tens Partners to make sums of 20.

17 + 3 = 20   14 + 6 = 20   15 + 5 = 20

Complete the missing Tens Partner to make 20.

16 + 4 = 20   11 + 9 = 20   8 + 12 = 20
18 + 2 = 20   13 + 7 = 20   6 + 14 = 20

Think Tens Partners to make Hundreds Partners.

90 + 10 = 100   80 + 20 = 100   70 + 30 = 100
60 + 40 = 100   50 + 50 = 100   40 + 60 = 100

Try these.

95 + 5 = 100   85 + 15 = 100   75 + 25 = 100
65 + 35 = 100   55 + 45 = 100   45 + 55 = 100
35 + 65 = 100   25 + 75 = 100   15 + 85 = 100
94 + 6 = 100   88 + 12 = 100   73 + 27 = 100

Page 15

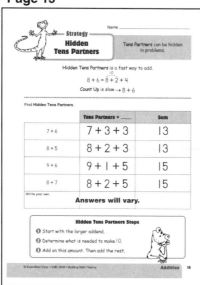

Strategy — Hidden Tens Partners
Tens Partners can be hidden in problems.

Hidden Tens Partners is a fast way to add.
8 + 6 = 8 + 2 + 4
Count Up is slow → 8 + 6

Find Hidden Tens Partners.

	Tens Partners + ___	Sum
7 + 6	7 + 3 + 3	13
8 + 5	8 + 2 + 3	13
9 + 6	9 + 1 + 5	15
8 + 7	8 + 2 + 5	15
Write your own.	**Answers will vary.**	

Hidden Tens Partners Steps
① Start with the larger addend.
② Determine what is needed to make 10.
③ Add on this amount. Then add the rest.

Page 16

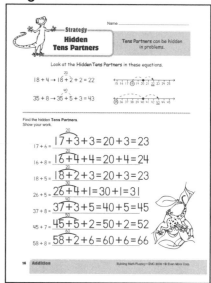

Strategy — Hidden Tens Partners
Tens Partners can be hidden in problems.

Look at the Hidden Tens Partners in these equations.
18 + 4 → 18 + 2 + 2 = 22
35 + 8 → 35 + 5 + 3 = 43

Find the hidden Tens Partners.
Show your work.

17 + 6 = 17 + 3 + 3 = 20 + 3 = 23
16 + 8 = 16 + 4 + 4 = 20 + 4 = 24
18 + 5 = 18 + 2 + 3 = 20 + 3 = 23
26 + 5 = 26 + 4 + 1 = 30 + 1 = 31
37 + 8 = 37 + 3 + 5 = 40 + 5 = 45
45 + 7 = 45 + 5 + 2 = 50 + 2 = 52
58 + 8 = 58 + 2 + 6 = 60 + 6 = 66

Page 17

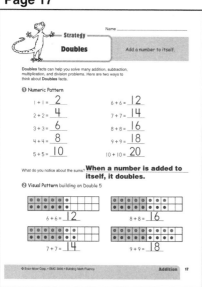

Strategy — Doubles
Add a number to itself.

Doubles facts can help you solve many addition, subtraction, multiplication, and division problems. Here are two ways to think about Doubles facts.

① Numeric Pattern

1 + 1 = 2   6 + 6 = 12
2 + 2 = 4   7 + 7 = 14
3 + 3 = 6   8 + 8 = 16
4 + 4 = 8   9 + 9 = 18
5 + 5 = 10   10 + 10 = 20

What do you notice about the sums? **When a number is added to itself, it doubles.**

② Visual Pattern building on Double 5

6 + 6 = 12   8 + 8 = 16
7 + 7 = 14   9 + 9 = 18

Page 18

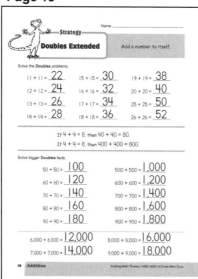

Strategy — Doubles Extended
Add a number to itself.

Solve the Doubles problems.

11 + 11 = 22   15 + 15 = 30   19 + 19 = 38
12 + 12 = 24   16 + 16 = 32   20 + 20 = 40
13 + 13 = 26   17 + 17 = 34   25 + 25 = 50
14 + 14 = 28   18 + 18 = 36   26 + 26 = 52

If 4 + 4 = 8, then 40 + 40 = 80.
If 4 + 4 = 8, then 400 + 400 = 800.

Solve bigger Doubles facts.

50 + 50 = 100   500 + 500 = 1,000
60 + 60 = 120   600 + 600 = 1,200
70 + 70 = 140   700 + 700 = 1,400
80 + 80 = 160   800 + 800 = 1,600
90 + 90 = 180   900 + 900 = 1,800

6,000 + 6,000 = 12,000   8,000 + 8,000 = 16,000
7,000 + 7,000 = 14,000   9,000 + 9,000 = 18,000

Page 19

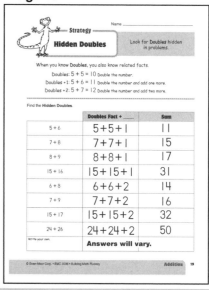

Strategy — Hidden Doubles
Look for Doubles hidden in problems.

When you know Doubles, you also know related facts.
Doubles: 5 + 5 = 10 double the number.
Doubles +1: 5 + 6 = 11 double the number and add one more.
Doubles +2: 5 + 7 = 12 double the number and add two more.

Find the Hidden Doubles.

	Doubles Fact + ___	Sum
5 + 6	5 + 5 + 1	11
7 + 8	7 + 7 + 1	15
8 + 9	8 + 8 + 1	17
15 + 16	15 + 15 + 1	31
6 + 8	6 + 6 + 2	14
7 + 9	7 + 7 + 2	16
15 + 17	15 + 15 + 2	32
24 + 26	24 + 24 + 2	50
Write your own.	**Answers will vary.**	

Page 20

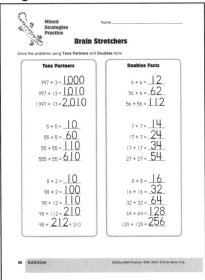

Mixed Strategies Practice

Brain Stretchers

Solve the problems using **Tens Partners** and **Doubles** facts.

Tens Partners	Doubles Facts
997 + 3 = 1,000	6 + 6 = 12
997 + 13 = 1,010	56 + 6 = 62
1,997 + 13 = 2,010	56 + 56 = 112
5 + 5 = 10	7 + 7 = 14
55 + 5 = 60	17 + 7 = 24
55 + 55 = 110	17 + 17 = 34
555 + 55 = 610	27 + 27 = 54
8 + 2 = 10	8 + 8 = 16
98 + 2 = 100	16 + 16 = 32
98 + 12 = 110	32 + 32 = 64
98 + 112 = 210	64 + 64 = 128
98 + 212 = 310	128 + 128 = 256

20 Addition

Page 21

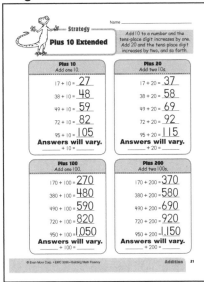

Strategy — Plus 10 Extended

Add 10 to a number and the tens-place digit increases by one. Add 20 and the tens-place digit increases by two, and so forth.

Plus 10 — Add one 10.
- 17 + 10 = 27
- 38 + 10 = 48
- 49 + 10 = 59
- 72 + 10 = 82
- 95 + 10 = 105
- **Answers will vary.** ___ + 10 =

Plus 20 — Add two 10s.
- 17 + 20 = 37
- 38 + 20 = 58
- 49 + 20 = 69
- 72 + 20 = 92
- 95 + 20 = 115
- **Answers will vary.** ___ + 20 =

Plus 100 — Add one 100.
- 170 + 100 = 270
- 380 + 100 = 480
- 490 + 100 = 590
- 720 + 100 = 820
- 950 + 100 = 1,050
- **Answers will vary.** ___ + 100 =

Plus 200 — Add two 100s.
- 170 + 200 = 370
- 380 + 200 = 580
- 490 + 200 = 690
- 720 + 200 = 920
- 950 + 200 = 1,150
- **Answers will vary.** ___ + 200 =

Addition 21

Page 22

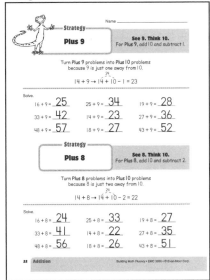

Strategy — Plus 9

See 9. Think 10. For Plus 9, add 10 and subtract 1.

Turn **Plus 9** problems into **Plus 10** problems because 9 is just one away from 10.

$14 + 9 \rightarrow 14 + 10 - 1 = 23$

Solve.
- 16 + 9 = 25   25 + 9 = 34   19 + 9 = 28
- 33 + 9 = 42   14 + 9 = 23   27 + 9 = 36
- 48 + 9 = 57   18 + 9 = 27   43 + 9 = 52

Strategy — Plus 8

See 8. Think 10. For Plus 8, add 10 and subtract 2.

Turn **Plus 8** problems into **Plus 10** problems because 8 is just two away from 10.

$14 + 8 \rightarrow 14 + 10 - 2 = 22$

Solve.
- 16 + 8 = 24   25 + 8 = 33   19 + 8 = 27
- 33 + 8 = 41   14 + 8 = 22   27 + 8 = 35
- 48 + 8 = 56   18 + 8 = 26   43 + 8 = 51

22 Addition

Page 23

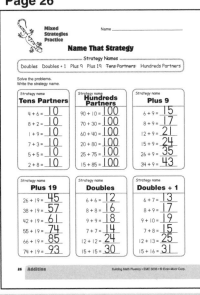

Strategy — Plus 19

See 19. Think 20. For Plus 19, add 20 and subtract 1.

Turn **Plus 19** problems into **Plus 20** problems because 19 is just one away from 20.

$14 + 19 \rightarrow 14 + 20 - 1 = 33$

Solve.
- 25 + 19 = 44   33 + 19 = 52   48 + 19 = 67
- 57 + 19 = 76   66 + 19 = 85   75 + 19 = 94

Strategy — Plus 99

See 99. Think 100. For Plus 99, add 100 and subtract 1.

Turn **Plus 99** problems into **Plus 100** problems because 99 is just one away from 100.

$140 + 99 \rightarrow 140 + 100 - 1 = 239$

Solve.
- 150 + 99 = 249   260 + 99 = 359   180 + 99 = 279
- 331 + 99 = 430   142 + 99 = 241   273 + 99 = 372

Write and solve a **Plus 99** problem of your own.

Answers will vary.

Addition 23

Page 24

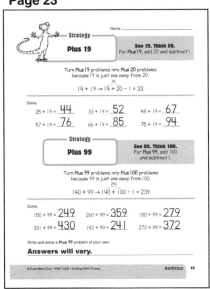

Mixed Strategies Practice

Brain Benders

Warm-up

17 +10 = 27	28 +9 = 37	45 +10 = 55	86 +9 = 95	34 +9 = 43

Complete each equation. Is it 9 or 10?
- 18 + 10 = 28   25 + 9 = 34   19 + 10 = 29
- 37 + 9 = 46   88 + 10 = 98   27 + 9 = 36

Write the missing addend. Is it 19 or 20?
- 22 + 20 = 42   48 + 19 = 67   31 + 19 = 50   31 + 20 = 51   65 + 19 = 84

Write the missing addend. Is it 99 or 100?
- 47 + 100 = 147   81 + 99 = 180   85 + 99 = 184   110 + 100 = 210   110 + 99 = 209

24 Addition

Page 25

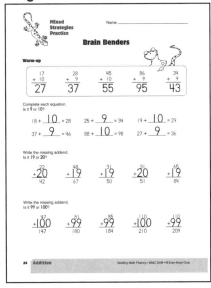

Mixed Strategies Practice

Many Ways to Add

8 + 6 = ?

Think about which strategy makes the problem easier for you to solve.

I see Tens Partners.
8 + 6 = 8 + 2 + 4 = 10 + 4 = 14

I see Doubles.
6 + 8 = 6 + 6 + 2 = 12 + 2 = 14

Think about the problems. Choose a strategy. Show your work.

What is your strategy for 17 + 9 =?
Answers will vary.
My strategy was ___

What is your strategy for 28 + 8 =?
Answers will vary.
My strategy was ___

Addition 25

Page 26

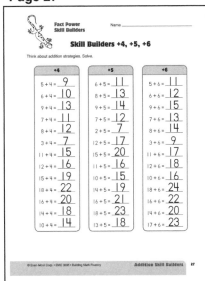

Mixed Strategies Practice

Name That Strategy

Strategy Names: Doubles   Doubles + 1   Plus 9   Plus 19   Tens Partners   Hundreds Partners

Solve the problems. Write the strategy name.

Strategy name — Tens Partners
- 4 + 6 = 10
- 8 + 2 = 10
- 1 + 9 = 10
- 7 + 3 = 10
- 5 + 5 = 10
- 2 + 8 = 10

Strategy name — Hundreds Partners
- 90 + 10 = 100
- 70 + 30 = 100
- 60 + 40 = 100
- 20 + 80 = 100
- 25 + 75 = 100
- 15 + 85 = 100

Strategy name — Plus 9
- 6 + 9 = 15
- 8 + 9 = 17
- 12 + 9 = 21
- 15 + 9 = 24
- 26 + 9 = 35
- 34 + 9 = 43

Strategy name — Plus 19
- 26 + 19 = 45
- 38 + 19 = 57
- 42 + 19 = 61
- 55 + 19 = 74
- 66 + 19 = 85
- 74 + 19 = 93

Strategy name — Doubles
- 6 + 6 = 12
- 8 + 8 = 16
- 9 + 9 = 18
- 7 + 7 = 14
- 12 + 12 = 24
- 15 + 15 = 30

Strategy name — Doubles + 1
- 6 + 7 = 13
- 8 + 9 = 17
- 9 + 10 = 19
- 7 + 8 = 15
- 12 + 13 = 25
- 15 + 16 = 31

26 Addition

Page 27

Fact Power Skill Builders

Skill Builders +4, +5, +6

Think about addition strategies. Solve.

+4	+5	+6
5 + 4 = 9	6 + 5 = 11	5 + 6 = 11
6 + 4 = 10	8 + 5 = 13	6 + 6 = 12
9 + 4 = 13	9 + 5 = 14	9 + 6 = 15
8 + 4 = 12	7 + 5 = 12	8 + 6 = 14
3 + 4 = 7	2 + 5 = 7	3 + 6 = 9
11 + 4 = 15	12 + 5 = 17	11 + 6 = 17
12 + 4 = 16	15 + 5 = 20	12 + 6 = 18
15 + 4 = 19	11 + 5 = 16	16 + 6 = 22
18 + 4 = 22	10 + 5 = 15	18 + 6 = 24
16 + 4 = 20	16 + 5 = 21	16 + 6 = 22
14 + 4 = 18	18 + 5 = 23	14 + 6 = 20
10 + 4 = 14	13 + 5 = 18	17 + 6 = 23

Addition Skill Builders 27

Page 28

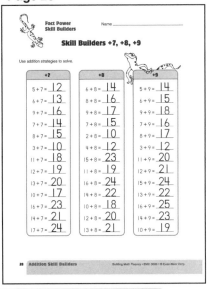

Fact Power Skill Builders

Skill Builders +7, +8, +9

Use addition strategies to solve.

+7	+8	+9
5 + 7 = 12	6 + 8 = 14	5 + 9 = 14
6 + 7 = 13	8 + 8 = 16	6 + 9 = 15
9 + 7 = 16	9 + 8 = 17	9 + 9 = 18
7 + 7 = 14	7 + 8 = 15	7 + 9 = 16
8 + 7 = 15	2 + 8 = 10	8 + 9 = 17
11 + 7 = 18	4 + 8 = 12	3 + 9 = 12
12 + 7 = 19	15 + 8 = 23	11 + 9 = 20
13 + 7 = 20	11 + 8 = 19	12 + 9 = 21
10 + 7 = 17	16 + 8 = 24	15 + 9 = 24
16 + 7 = 23	14 + 8 = 22	13 + 9 = 22
14 + 7 = 21	10 + 8 = 18	16 + 9 = 25
17 + 7 = 24	12 + 8 = 20	14 + 9 = 23
	13 + 8 = 21	10 + 9 = 19

28 Addition Skill Builders

Page 29

Name _____

Skip Count by 10

Skip Count up by 10s to practice adding 10 to a number.

Skip Count back by 10s to practice subtracting 10 from a number.

Use the number chart.

1	2	3	4	5	6	7	8	9	10
11	12	13	14	15	16	17	18	19	20
21	22	23	24	25	26	27	28	29	30
31	32	33	34	35	36	37	38	39	40
41	42	43	44	45	46	47	48	49	50
51	52	53	54	55	56	57	58	59	60

Start at 4. Skip Count up by 10s.
4, 14, 24, 34, 44, 54, 64, 74, 84, 94, 104, 114, 124, 134

Start at 154. Skip Count back by 10s.
164, 154, 144, 134, 124, 114, 104, 94, 84, 74, 64, 54, 44, 34

Start at 6. Skip Count up by 10s.
6, 16, 26, 36, 46, 56, 66, 76, 86, 96, 106, 116, 126, 136

Start at 176. Skip Count back by 10s.
176, 166, 156, 146, 136, 126, 116, 106, 96, 86, 76, 66, 56

Start at 17. Skip Count up by 10s.
17, 27, 37, 47, 57, 67, 77, 87, 97, 107, 117, 127, 137

Start at 147. Skip Count back by 10s.
147, 137, 127, 117, 107, 97, 87, 77, 67, 57, 47, 37, 27, 17

Page 30

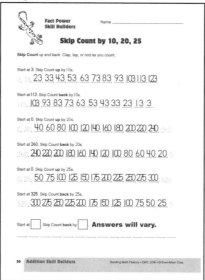

Name _____

Skip Count by 10, 20, 25

Skip Count up and back. Clap, tap, or nod as you count.

Start at 3. Skip Count up by 10s.
3, 13, 23, 33, 43, 53, 63, 73, 83, 93, 103, 113, 123

Start at 113. Skip Count back by 10s.
113, 103, 93, 83, 73, 63, 53, 43, 33, 23, 13, 3

Start at 0. Skip Count up by 20s.
0, 20, 40, 60, 80, 100, 120, 140, 160, 180, 200, 220, 240

Start at 260. Skip Count back by 20s.
260, 240, 220, 200, 180, 160, 140, 120, 100, 80, 60, 40, 20, 0

Start at 0. Skip Count up by 25s.
0, 25, 50, 75, 100, 125, 150, 175, 200, 225, 250, 275, 300

Start at 325. Skip Count back by 25s.
325, 300, 275, 250, 225, 200, 175, 150, 125, 100, 75, 50, 25, 0

Start at ☐ Skip Count back by ☐ **Answers will vary.**

Page 31

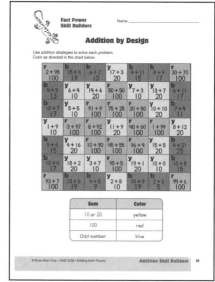

Name _____

Addition by Design

Use addition strategies to solve each problem.
Color as directed in the chart below.

r 2 + 98 100	y 15 + 4	b 6 + 7 13	y 17 + 3 20	b 4 + 11	b 8 + 9 17	y 30 + 70 100
b	r 12 + 8 20	y 14 + 6 10	r 50 + 50 100	y 7 + 3 10	b 13 + 7 20	r 6 + 11
r 10 + 7 17	y 5 + 5	y 91 + 9 100	r 75 + 25	y 20 + 80 100	r 10 + 10 20	y 7 + 4
y 1 + 9 10	b 3 + 97 100	b 8 + 92	y 11 + 9	r 40 + 60 100	r 1 + 99 100	b 8 + 12 20
y 9 + 6 15	r 4 + 16 20	b 10 + 90 100	r 45 + 55	y 96 + 4	b 15 + 5 20	r 4 + 21
b 13 + 4	b 18 + 2	y 3 + 7 10	y 95 + 5	y 19 + 1 20	r 10 + 0	b 10 + 8
r 93 + 7 100	y 13 + 6	b 4 + 5	r 2 + 8 10	b 10 + 9	r 2 + 3	b 94 + 6 100

Sum	Color
10 or 20	yellow
100	red
Odd number	blue

Page 34

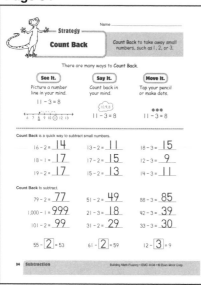

Strategy

Count Back

Count Back to take away small numbers, such as 1, 2, or 3.

There are many ways to Count Back.

See It. Picture a number line in your mind.
11 − 3 = 8

Say It. Count back in your mind.
11 − 3 = 8

Move It. Tap your pencil or make dots.
11 − 3 = 8

Count Back is a quick way to subtract small numbers.

16 − 2 = 14   13 − 2 = 11   18 − 3 = 15
18 − 1 = 17   17 − 2 = 15   12 − 3 = 9
19 − 2 = 17   15 − 2 = 13   14 − 3 = 11

Count Back to subtract.

79 − 2 = 77   51 − 2 = 49   88 − 3 = 85
1,000 − 1 = 999   21 − 3 = 18   42 − 3 = 39
101 − 2 = 99   31 − 2 = 29   33 − 3 = 30

55 − [2] = 53   61 − [2] = 59   12 − [3] = 9

Page 35

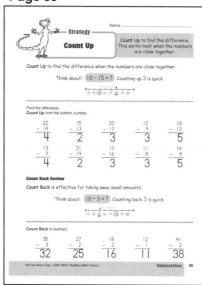

Strategy

Count Up

Count Up to find the difference. This works best when the numbers are close together.

Count Up to find the difference when the numbers are close together.

Think about: 18 − 15 = ? Counting up 3 is quick.

13 14 (15) 16 17 18 19 20

Find the difference.
Count Up from the bottom number.

| 22 − 18 = 4 | 15 − 13 = 2 | 20 − 17 = 3 | 12 − 9 = 3 | 18 − 13 = 5 |
| 13 − 9 = 4 | 21 − 19 = 2 | 19 − 16 = 3 | 11 − 8 = 3 | 14 − 9 = 5 |

Count Back Review

Count Back is effective for taking away small amounts.

Think about: 18 − 3 = ? Counting back 3 is quick.

13 14 (15) 16 17 (18) 19 20

Count Back to subtract.

| 35 − 3 = 32 | 27 − 2 = 25 | 18 − 2 = 16 | 12 − 1 = 11 | 41 − 3 = 38 |

Page 36

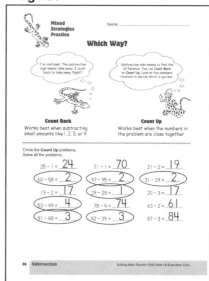

Name _____

Which Way?

I'm confused. The subtraction sign means take away. I count back to take away. Right?

Subtraction also means to find the difference. You can Count Back or Count Up. Look at the numbers involved to decide which is quicker.

Count Back Works best when subtracting small amounts like 1, 2, 3, or 4

Count Up Works best when the numbers in the problem are close together

Circle the Count Up problems.
Solve all the problems.

25 − 1 = 24   71 − 1 = 70   21 − 2 = 19
(60 − 58 = 2)   (97 − 95 = 2)   31 − 29 = 2
19 − 2 = 17   29 − 28 = 1   20 − 3 = 17
(53 − 49 = 4)   78 − 4 = 74   63 − 2 = 61
(91 − 88 = 3)   (42 − 39 = 3)   87 − 3 = 84

Page 37

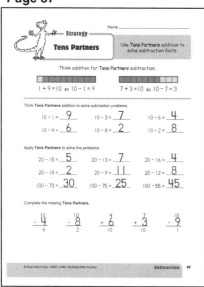

Strategy

Tens Partners

Use Tens Partners addition to solve subtraction facts.

Think addition for Tens Partners subtraction.

1 + 9 = 10 so 10 − 1 = 9   7 + 3 = 10 so 10 − 7 = 3

Think Tens Partners addition to solve subtraction problems.

10 − 1 = 9   10 − 3 = 7   10 − 6 = 4
10 − 4 = 6   10 − 8 = 2   10 − 2 = 8

Apply Tens Partners to solve the problems.

20 − 15 = 5   20 − 13 = 7   20 − 16 = 4
20 − 18 = 2   20 − 9 = 11   20 − 12 = 8
100 − 70 = 30 100 − 75 = 25 100 − 55 = 45

Complete the missing Tens Partners.

| − 10 / 4 = 6 | − 10 / 8 = 2 | + 4 / 6 = 10 | + 7 / 3 = 10 | − 10 / 9 = 1 |

Page 38

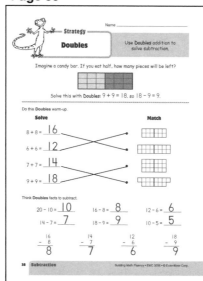

Strategy

Doubles

Use Doubles addition to solve subtraction.

Imagine a candy bar. If you eat half, how many pieces will be left?

Solve this with Doubles: 9 + 9 = 18, so 18 − 9 = 9.

Do this Doubles warm-up.

Solve   **Match**
8 + 8 = 16
6 + 6 = 12
7 + 7 = 14
9 + 9 = 18

Think Doubles facts to subtract.

20 − 10 = 10   16 − 8 = 8   12 − 6 = 6
14 − 7 = 7   18 − 9 = 9   10 − 5 = 5

| 16 − 8 = 8 | 14 − 7 = 7 | 12 − 6 = 6 | 18 − 9 = 9 |

Page 39

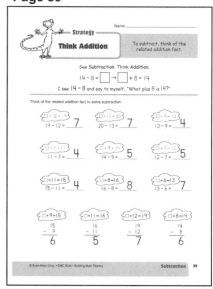

Strategy

Think Addition

To subtract, think of the related addition fact.

See Subtraction. Think Addition.

14 − 8 = ☐ → ☐ + 8 = 14

I see 14 − 8 and say to myself, "What plus 8 is 14?"

Think of the related addition fact to solve subtraction.

☐ + 12 = 19   ☐ + 13 = 20   ☐ + 9 = 13
19 − 12 = 7   20 − 13 = 7   13 − 9 = 4

☐ + 7 = 11   ☐ + 9 = 14   ☐ + 7 = 12
11 − 7 = 4   14 − 9 = 5   12 − 7 = 5

☐ + 11 = 15   ☐ + 8 = 16   ☐ + 6 = 13
15 − 11 = 4   16 − 8 = 8   13 − 6 = 7

☐ + 9 = 15   ☐ + 11 = 16   ☐ + 12 = 19   ☐ + 8 = 14
15 − 9 = 6   16 − 11 = 5   19 − 12 = 7   14 − 8 = 6

Page 40

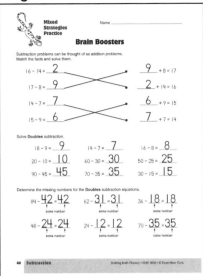

Mixed Strategies Practice

Brain Boosters

Name _____

Subtraction problems can be thought of as addition problems. Match the facts and solve them.

16 – 14 = **2**   9 + 8 = 17
17 – 8 = **9**   2 + 14 = 16
14 – 7 = **7**   6 + 9 = 15
15 – 9 = **6**   7 + 7 = 14

Solve **Doubles** subtraction.

18 – 9 = **9**   14 – 7 = **7**   16 – 8 = **8**
20 – 10 = **10**   60 – 30 = **30**   50 – 25 = **25**
90 – 45 = **45**   70 – 35 = **35**   30 – 15 = **15**

Determine the missing numbers for the **Doubles** subtraction equations.

84 – **42** = **42**   62 – **31** = **31**   36 – **18** = **18**
      same number   same number   same number

48 – **24** = **24**   24 – **12** = **12**   70 – **35** = **35**
      some number   some number   same number

40   Subtraction

Page 41

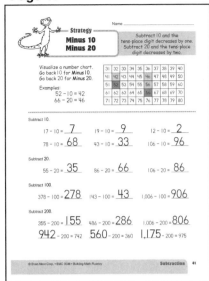

Strategy

Minus 10 Minus 20

Name _____

Subtract 10 and the tens-place digit decreases by one. Subtract 20 and the tens-place digit decreases by two.

Visualize a number chart.
Go back 10 for **Minus 10**.
Go back 20 for **Minus 20**.

Examples:
52 – 10 = 42
66 – 20 = 46

Subtract 10.

17 – 10 = **7**   19 – 10 = **9**   12 – 10 = **2**
78 – 10 = **68**   43 – 10 = **33**   106 – 10 = **96**

Subtract 20.

55 – 20 = **35**   86 – 20 = **66**   106 – 20 = **86**

Subtract 100.

378 – 100 = **278**   143 – 100 = **43**   1,006 – 100 = **906**

Subtract 200.

355 – 200 = **155**   486 – 200 = **286**   1,006 – 200 = **806**
942 – 200 = 742   560 – 200 = 360   1,175 – 200 = 975

Subtraction   41

Page 42

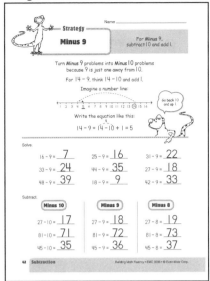

Strategy

Minus 9

Name _____

For Minus 9, subtract 10 and add 1.

Turn Minus 9 problems into Minus 10 problems because 9 is just one away from 10.

For 14 – 9, think 14 – 10 and add 1.

Imagine a number line:

Go back 10 and up 1

Write the equation like this:
14 – 9 = 14 – 10 + 1 = 5

Solve.

16 – 9 = **7**   25 – 9 = **16**   31 – 9 = **22**
33 – 9 = **24**   44 – 9 = **35**   27 – 9 = **18**
48 – 9 = **39**   18 – 9 = **9**   42 – 9 = **33**

Subtract.

Minus 10	Minus 9	Minus 8
27 – 10 = **17**	27 – 9 = **18**	27 – 8 = **19**
81 – 10 = **71**	81 – 9 = **72**	81 – 8 = **73**
45 – 10 = **35**	45 – 9 = **36**	45 – 8 = **37**

42   Subtraction

Page 43

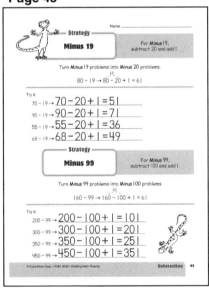

Strategy

Minus 19

Name _____

For Minus 19, subtract 20 and add 1.

Turn Minus 19 problems into Minus 20 problems.
80 – 19 → 80 – 20 + 1 = 61

Try it.
70 – 19 → **70 – 20 + 1 = 51**
90 – 19 → **90 – 20 + 1 = 71**
55 – 19 → **55 – 20 + 1 = 36**
68 – 19 → **68 – 20 + 1 = 49**

Strategy

Minus 99

For Minus 99, subtract 100 and add 1.

Turn Minus 99 problems into Minus 100 problems.
160 – 99 → 160 – 100 + 1 = 61

Try it.
200 – 99 → **200 – 100 + 1 = 101**
300 – 99 → **300 – 100 + 1 = 201**
350 – 99 → **350 – 100 + 1 = 251**
450 – 99 → **450 – 100 + 1 = 351**

Subtraction   43

Page 44

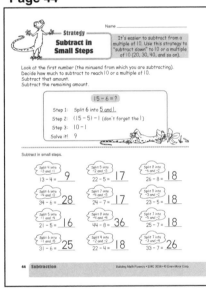

Strategy

Subtract in Small Steps

Name _____

It's easier to subtract from a multiple of 10. Use this strategy to "subtract down" to 10 or a multiple of 10 (20, 30, 40, and so on).

Look at the first number (the minuend from which you are subtracting). Decide how much to subtract to reach 10 or a multiple of 10. Subtract that amount. Subtract the remaining amount.

15 – 6 = ?

Step 1: Split 6 into 5 and 1.
Step 2: (15 – 5) – 1 (don't forget the 1)
Step 3: 10 – 1
Solve it! 9

Subtract in small steps.

Split 4 into -3 and -1
13 – 4 = **9**

Split 5 into -2 and -3
22 – 5 = **17**

Split 8 into -6 and -2
26 – 8 = **18**

Split 6 into -4 and -2
34 – 6 = **28**

Split 7 into -4 and -3
24 – 7 = **17**

Split 5 into -3 and -2
23 – 5 = **18**

Split 5 into -1 and -4
21 – 5 = **16**

Split 8 into -4 and -4
44 – 8 = **36**

Split 7 into -5 and -2
25 – 7 = **18**

Split 6 into -1 and -5
31 – 6 = **25**

Split 4 into -2 and -2
22 – 4 = **18**

Split 7 into -3 and -4
33 – 7 = **26**

44   Subtraction

Page 45

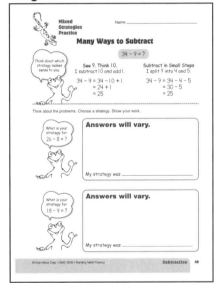

Mixed Strategies Practice

Many Ways to Subtract

Name _____

34 – 9 = ?

Think about which strategy makes sense to you.

See 9. Think 10.
I subtract 10 and add 1.
34 – 9 = 34 – 10 + 1
= 24 + 1
= 25

Subtract in Small Steps
I split 9 into 4 and 5.
34 – 9 = 34 – 4 – 5
= 30 – 5
= 25

Think about the problems. Choose a strategy. Show your work.

What is your strategy for 26 – 8 = ?

Answers will vary.

My strategy was _____

What is your strategy for 18 – 9 = ?

Answers will vary.

My strategy was _____

Subtraction   45

Page 46

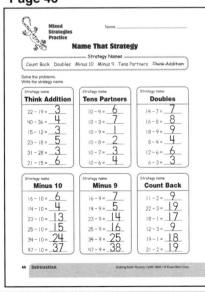

Mixed Strategies Practice

Name That Strategy

Name _____

Strategy Names

Count Back   Doubles   Minus 10   Minus 9   Tens Partners   ~~Think Addition~~

Solve the problems.
Write the strategy name.

Strategy name
Think Addition
22 – 19 = **3**
40 – 36 = **4**
15 – 12 = **3**
23 – 18 = **5**
31 – 28 = **3**
21 – 15 = **6**

Strategy name
Tens Partners
10 – 4 = **6**
10 – 3 = **7**
10 – 9 = **1**
10 – 7 = **3**
10 – 6 = **4**

Strategy name
Doubles
14 – 7 = **7**
16 – 8 = **8**
18 – 9 = **9**
8 – 4 = **4**
12 – 6 = **6**

Strategy name
Minus 10
16 – 10 = **6**
14 – 10 = **4**
23 – 10 = **13**
25 – 10 = **15**
34 – 10 = **24**
47 – 10 = **37**

Strategy name
Minus 9
16 – 9 = **7**
14 – 9 = **5**
23 – 9 = **14**
25 – 9 = **16**
34 – 9 = **25**
47 – 9 = **38**

Strategy name
Count Back
11 – 2 = **9**
22 – 3 = **19**
18 – 1 = **17**
12 – 3 = **9**
19 – 1 = **18**
21 – 2 = **19**

46   Subtraction

Page 47

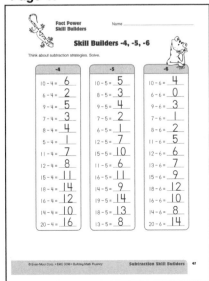

Fact Power Skill Builders

Skill Builders -4, -5, -6

Name _____

Think about subtraction strategies. Solve.

-4	-5	-6
10 – 4 = **6**	10 – 5 = **5**	10 – 6 = **4**
6 – 4 = **2**	8 – 5 = **3**	6 – 6 = **0**
9 – 4 = **5**	9 – 5 = **4**	9 – 6 = **3**
7 – 4 = **3**	7 – 5 = **2**	7 – 6 = **1**
8 – 4 = **4**	6 – 5 = **1**	8 – 6 = **2**
5 – 4 = **1**	12 – 5 = **7**	11 – 6 = **5**
11 – 4 = **7**	15 – 5 = **10**	12 – 6 = **6**
12 – 4 = **8**	11 – 5 = **6**	13 – 6 = **7**
18 – 4 = **14**	14 – 5 = **9**	18 – 6 = **12**
16 – 4 = **12**	19 – 5 = **14**	16 – 6 = **10**
14 – 4 = **10**	18 – 5 = **13**	14 – 6 = **8**
20 – 4 = **16**	13 – 5 = **8**	20 – 6 = **14**

Subtraction Skill Builders   47

Page 48

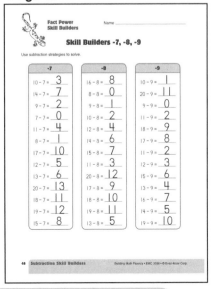

Fact Power Skill Builders

Skill Builders -7, -8, -9

Name _____

Use subtraction strategies to solve.

-7	-8	-9
10 – 7 = **3**	16 – 8 = **8**	10 – 9 = **1**
14 – 7 = **7**	8 – 8 = **0**	20 – 9 = **11**
7 – 7 = **0**	11 – 8 = **3**	9 – 9 = **0**
7 – 7 = **0**	10 – 8 = **2**	11 – 9 = **2**
11 – 7 = **4**	12 – 8 = **4**	18 – 9 = **9**
8 – 7 = **1**	14 – 8 = **6**	17 – 9 = **8**
17 – 7 = **10**	15 – 8 = **7**	11 – 9 = **2**
12 – 7 = **5**	20 – 8 = **12**	15 – 9 = **6**
13 – 7 = **6**	13 – 8 = **5**	13 – 9 = **4**
18 – 7 = **11**	18 – 8 = **10**	16 – 9 = **7**
19 – 7 = **12**	19 – 8 = **11**	14 – 9 = **5**
15 – 7 = **8**	13 – 8 = **5**	19 – 9 = **10**

48   Subtraction Skill Builders

Page 50

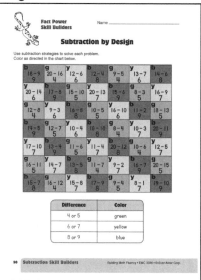

Fact Power Skill Builders Name _____

Subtraction by Design

Use subtraction strategies to solve each problem.
Color as directed in the chart below.

Difference	Color
4 or 5	green
6 or 7	yellow
8 or 9	blue

Page 53

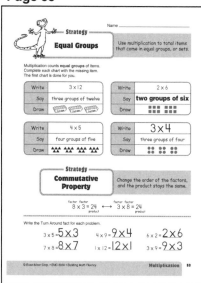

— Strategy —
Equal Groups   Use multiplication to total items that come in equal groups, or sets.

Multiplication counts **equal groups** of items.
Complete each chart with the missing item.
The first chart is done for you.

Write	3 × 12		Write	2 × 6
Say	three groups of twelve		Say	**two groups of six**
Draw			Draw	

Write	4 × 5		Write	3 × 4
Say	four groups of five		Say	three groups of four
Draw			Draw	

— Strategy —
Commutative Property   Change the order of the factors, and the product stays the same.

factor factor   factor factor
8 × 3 = 24   3 × 8 = 24
      product   product

Write the Turn Around fact for each problem.

3 × 5 = **5 × 3**   4 × 9 = **9 × 4**   6 × 2 = **2 × 6**
7 × 8 = **8 × 7**   1 × 12 = **12 × 1**   3 × 9 = **9 × 3**

Page 54

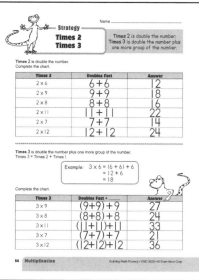

— Strategy —
Times 2 Times 3   Times 2 is double the number. Times 3 is double the number plus one more group of the number.

Times 2 is double the number.
Complete the chart.

Times 2	Doubles Fact	Answer
2 × 6	6 + 6	12
2 × 9	9 + 9	18
2 × 8	8 + 8	16
2 × 11	11 + 11	22
2 × 7	7 + 7	14
2 × 12	12 + 12	24

Times 3 is double the number plus one more group of the number.
Times 3 = Times 2 + Times 1.

Example: 3 × 6 = (6 + 6) + 6
= 12 + 6
= 18

Complete the chart.

Times 3	Doubles Fact + ___	Answer
3 × 9	(9 + 9) + 9	27
3 × 8	(8 + 8) + 8	24
3 × 11	(11 + 11) + 11	33
3 × 7	(7 + 7) + 7	21
3 × 12	(12 + 12) + 12	36

Page 55

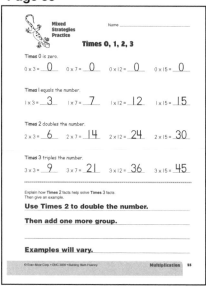

Mixed Strategies Practice   Name _____

Times 0, 1, 2, 3

Times 0 is zero.

0 × 3 = **0**   0 × 7 = **0**   0 × 12 = **0**   0 × 15 = **0**

Times 1 equals the number.

1 × 3 = **3**   1 × 7 = **7**   1 × 12 = **12**   1 × 15 = **15**

Times 2 doubles the number.

2 × 3 = **6**   2 × 7 = **14**   2 × 12 = **24**   2 × 15 = **30**

Times 3 triples the number.

3 × 3 = **9**   3 × 7 = **21**   3 × 12 = **36**   3 × 15 = **45**

Explain how Times 2 facts help solve Times 3 facts.
Then give an example.

Use Times 2 to double the number.

Then add one more group.

Examples will vary.

Page 56

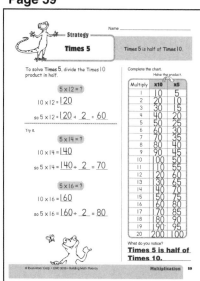

— Strategy —
Times 4   Times 4 is Times 2 + Times 2.

Times 4 is four sets of the number.
Put the four sets in two groups for easier computation.

Four sets: 4 × 6 = ▦ ▦ ▦ ▦ = 24
          6 + 6 + 6 + 6

Two groups: 4 × 6 = ▦ ▦ = 24
           12 + 12

Or think of it like this:

4 × 6 = 6 + 6 + 6 + 6 = 24

Put the four sets in two groups for easier computation.
Circle the two groups and solve.

4 × 5 = 5 + 5 + 5 + 5 = **20**

4 × 7 = 7 + 7 + 7 + 7 = **28**

4 × 8 = 8 + 8 + 8 + 8 = **32**

4 × 9 = 9 + 9 + 9 + 9 = **36**

4 × 12 = 12 + 12 + 12 + 12 = **48**

Page 57

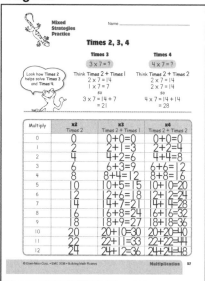

Mixed Strategies Practice   Name _____

Times 2, 3, 4

	Times 3	Times 4
	3 × 7 = ?	4 × 7 = ?

Look how Times 2 helps solve Times 3 and Times 4.

Think Times 2 + Times 1
2 × 7 = 14
1 × 7 = 7
so
3 × 7 = 14 + 7
= 21

Think Times 2 + Times 2
2 × 7 = 14
2 × 7 = 14
so
4 × 7 = 14 + 14
= 28

Multiply	x2 Times 2	x3 Times 2 + Times 1	x4 Times 2 + Times 2
0	0	0 + 0 = 0	0 + 0 = 0
1	2	2 + 1 = 3	2 + 2 = 4
2	4	4 + 2 = 6	4 + 4 = 8
3	6	6 + 3 = 9	6 + 6 = 12
4	8	8 + 4 = 12	8 + 8 = 16
5	10	10 + 5 = 15	10 + 10 = 20
6	12	12 + 6 = 18	12 + 12 = 24
7	14	14 + 7 = 21	14 + 14 = 28
8	16	16 + 8 = 24	16 + 16 = 32
9	18	18 + 9 = 27	18 + 18 = 36
10	20	20 + 10 = 30	20 + 20 = 40
11	22	22 + 11 = 33	22 + 22 = 44
12	24	24 + 12 = 36	24 + 24 = 48

Page 58

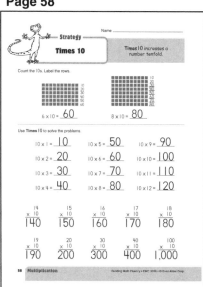

— Strategy —
Times 10   Times 10 increases a number tenfold.

Count the 10s. Label the rows.

6 × 10 = **60**   8 × 10 = **80**

Use Times 10 to solve the problems.

10 × 1 = **10**   10 × 5 = **50**   10 × 9 = **90**
10 × 2 = **20**   10 × 6 = **60**   10 × 10 = **100**
10 × 3 = **30**   10 × 7 = **70**   10 × 11 = **110**
10 × 4 = **40**   10 × 8 = **80**   10 × 12 = **120**

| 14 × 10 = **140** | 15 × 10 = **150** | 16 × 10 = **160** | 17 × 10 = **170** | 18 × 10 = **180** |
| 19 × 10 = **190** | 20 × 10 = **200** | 30 × 10 = **300** | 40 × 10 = **400** | 100 × 10 = **1,000** |

Page 59

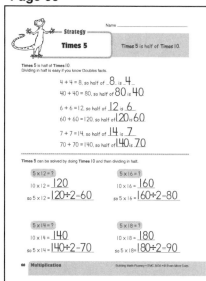

— Strategy —
Times 5   Times 5 is half of Times 10.

To solve Times 5, divide the Times 10 product in half.

5 × 12 = ?
10 × 12 = 120
so 5 × 12 = 120 ÷ 2 = **60**

Try it.

5 × 14 = ?
10 × 14 = **140**
so 5 × 14 = 140 ÷ 2 = **70**

5 × 16 = ?
10 × 16 = **160**
so 5 × 16 = 160 ÷ 2 = **80**

Complete the chart.
Halve the product.

Multiply	x10	x5
1	10	5
2	20	10
3	30	15
4	40	20
5	50	25
6	60	30
7	70	35
8	80	40
9	90	45
10	100	50
11	110	55
12	120	60
13	130	65
14	140	70
15	150	75
16	160	80
17	170	85
18	180	90
19	190	95
20	200	100

What do you notice?
Times 5 is half of Times 10.

Page 60

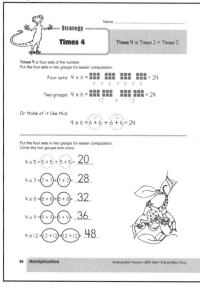

— Strategy —
Times 5   Times 5 is half of Times 10.

Times 5 is half of Times 10.
Dividing in half is easy if you know Doubles facts.

4 + 4 = 8, so half of **8** is **4**
40 + 40 = 80, so half of **80** is **40**

6 + 6 = 12, so half of **12** is **6**
60 + 60 = 120, so half of **120** is **60**

7 + 7 = 14, so half of **14** is **7**
70 + 70 = 140, so half of **140** is **70**

Times 5 can be solved by doing Times 10 and then dividing in half.

5 × 12 = ?
10 × 12 = **120**
so 5 × 12 = **120 ÷ 2 = 60**

5 × 16 = ?
10 × 16 = **160**
so 5 × 16 = **160 ÷ 2 = 80**

5 × 14 = ?
10 × 14 = **140**
so 5 × 14 = **140 ÷ 2 = 70**

5 × 18 = ?
10 × 18 = **180**
so 5 × 18 = **180 ÷ 2 = 90**

Page 61

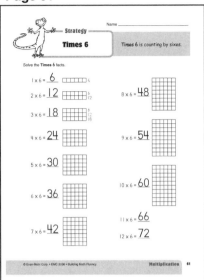

Page 62

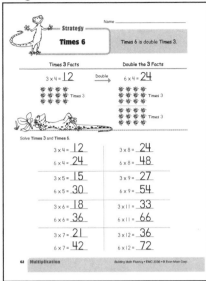

Page 63

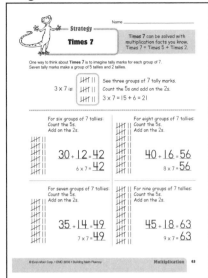

Page 64

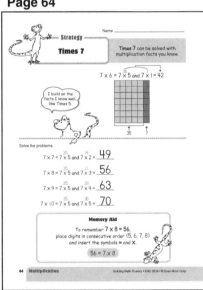

Page 65

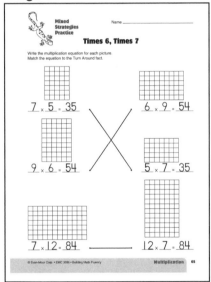

Page 66

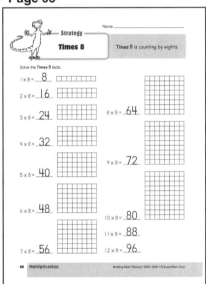

Page 67

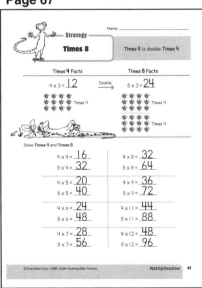

Page 68

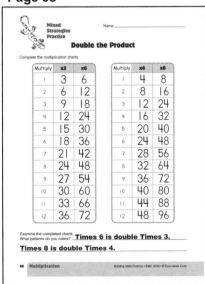

Page 69

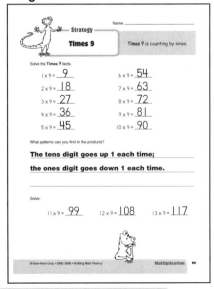

Page 70

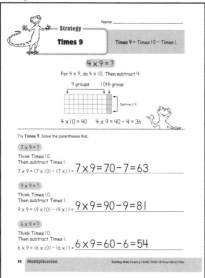

Strategy
Times 9 Times 9 = Times 10 – Times 1.

$4 \times 9 = ?$

For 4×9, do 4×10. Then subtract 4.

9 groups | 10th group

Subtract 4

$4 \times 10 = 40$ $4 \times 9 = 40 - 4 = 36$

Try **Times 9**. Solve the parentheses first.

$7 \times 9 = ?$
Think Times 10.
Then subtract Times 1.
$7 \times 9 = (7 \times 10) - (7 \times 1)$ $7 \times 9 = 70 - 7 = 63$

$9 \times 9 = ?$
Think Times 10.
Then subtract Times 1.
$9 \times 9 = (9 \times 10) - (9 \times 1)$ $9 \times 9 = 90 - 9 = 81$

$6 \times 9 = ?$
Think Times 10.
Then subtract Times 1.
$6 \times 9 = (6 \times 10) - (6 \times 1)$ $6 \times 9 = 60 - 6 = 54$

70 Multiplication   Building Math Fluency EMC 3036 • © Evan-Moor Corp.

Page 71

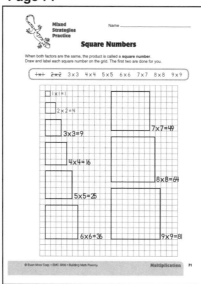

Mixed Strategies Practice

Square Numbers

When both factors are the same, the product is called a **square number**. Draw and label each square number on the grid. The first two are done for you.

1×1 2×2 3×3 4×4 5×5 6×6 7×7 8×8 9×9

1×1
$2 \times 2 = 4$
$3 \times 3 = 9$
$7 \times 7 = 49$
$4 \times 4 = 16$
$8 \times 8 = 64$
$5 \times 5 = 25$
$6 \times 6 = 36$ $9 \times 9 = 81$

© Evan-Moor Corp. • EMC 3036 • Building Math Fluency   Multiplication 71

Page 72

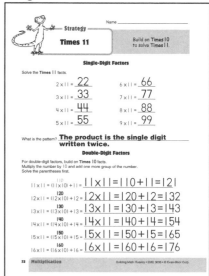

Strategy
Times 11 Build on Times 10 to solve Times 11.

Single-Digit Factors

Solve the **Times 11** facts.

$2 \times 11 = 22$ $6 \times 11 = 66$
$3 \times 11 = 33$ $7 \times 11 = 77$
$4 \times 11 = 44$ $8 \times 11 = 88$
$5 \times 11 = 55$ $9 \times 11 = 99$

What is the pattern? **The product is the single digit written twice.**

Double-Digit Factors

For double-digit factors, build on **Times 10** facts.
Multiply the number by 10 and add one more group of the number.
Solve the parentheses first.

$11 \times 11 = (11 \times 10) + 11 = 11 \times 11 = 110 + 11 = 121$
$12 \times 11 = (12 \times 10) + 12 = 12 \times 11 = 120 + 12 = 132$
$13 \times 11 = (13 \times 10) + 13 = 13 \times 11 = 130 + 13 = 143$
$14 \times 11 = (14 \times 10) + 14 = 14 \times 11 = 140 + 14 = 154$
$15 \times 11 = (15 \times 10) + 15 = 15 \times 11 = 150 + 15 = 165$
$16 \times 11 = (16 \times 10) + 16 = 16 \times 11 = 160 + 16 = 176$

72 Multiplication   Building Math Fluency • EMC 3036 • © Evan-Moor Corp.

Page 73

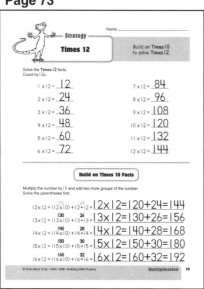

Strategy
Times 12 Build on Times 10 to solve Times 12.

Solve the **Times 12** facts.
Count by 12s.

$1 \times 12 = 12$ $7 \times 12 = 84$
$2 \times 12 = 24$ $8 \times 12 = 96$
$3 \times 12 = 36$ $9 \times 12 = 108$
$4 \times 12 = 48$ $10 \times 12 = 120$
$5 \times 12 = 60$ $11 \times 12 = 132$
$6 \times 12 = 72$ $12 \times 12 = 144$

Build on Times 10 Facts

Multiply the number by 10 and add two more groups of the number.
Solve the parentheses first.

$12 \times 12 = (12 \times 10) + 12 + 12 = 12 \times 12 = 120 + 24 = 144$
$13 \times 12 = (13 \times 10) + 13 + 13 = 13 \times 12 = 130 + 26 = 156$
$14 \times 12 = (14 \times 10) + 14 + 14 = 14 \times 12 = 140 + 28 = 168$
$15 \times 12 = (15 \times 10) + 15 + 15 = 15 \times 12 = 150 + 30 = 180$
$16 \times 12 = (16 \times 10) + 16 + 16 = 16 \times 12 = 160 + 32 = 192$

© Evan-Moor Corp. • EMC 3036 • Building Math Fluency   Multiplication 73

Page 74

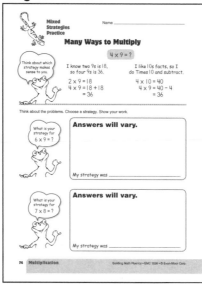

Mixed Strategies Practice

Many Ways to Multiply

$4 \times 9 = ?$

Think about which strategy makes sense to you.

I know two 9s is 18, so four 9s is 36.
$2 \times 9 = 18$
$4 \times 9 = 18 + 18 = 36$

I like 10s facts, so I do Times 10 and subtract.
$4 \times 10 = 40$
$4 \times 9 = 40 - 4 = 36$

Think about the problems. Choose a strategy. Show your work.

What is your strategy for $6 \times 9 = ?$
Answers will vary.
My strategy was

What is your strategy for $7 \times 8 = ?$
Answers will vary.
My strategy was

74 Multiplication   Building Math Fluency • EMC 3036 • © Evan-Moor Corp.

Page 75

Mixed Strategies Practice

100 Products

Complete the chart.

×	1	2	3	4	5	6	7	8	9	10
1	1	2	3	4	5	6	7	8	9	10
2	2	4	6	8	10	12	14	16	18	20
3	3	6	9	12	15	18	21	24	27	30
4	4	8	12	16	20	24	28	32	36	40
5	5	10	15	20	25	30	35	40	45	50
6	6	12	18	24	30	36	42	48	54	60
7	7	14	21	28	35	42	49	56	63	70
8	8	16	24	32	40	48	56	64	72	80
9	9	18	27	36	45	54	63	72	81	90
10	10	20	30	40	50	60	70	80	90	100

Square numbers have the same factors (1×1, 2×2, 3×3, etc.).
Shade the boxes with square products in yellow.

Challenge: Which two square numbers total 100?
$64 + 36 = 100$

© Evan-Moor Corp. • EMC 3036 • Building Math Fluency   Multiplication 75

Page 76

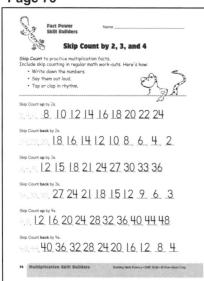

Fact Power Skill Builders

Skip Count by 2, 3, and 4

Skip Count to practice multiplication facts.
Include skip counting in regular math work-outs. Here's how:
• Write down the numbers.
• Say them out loud.
• Tap or clap in rhythm.

Skip Count up by 2s.
2, 4, 6, 8, 10, 12, 14, 16, 18, 20, 22, 24

Skip Count back by 2s.
24, 22, 20, 18, 16, 14, 12, 10, 8, 6, 4, 2

Skip Count up by 3s.
3, 6, 9, 12, 15, 18, 21, 24, 27, 30, 33, 36

Skip Count back by 3s.
36, 33, 30, 27, 24, 21, 18, 15, 12, 9, 6, 3

Skip Count up by 4s.
4, 8, 12, 16, 20, 24, 28, 32, 36, 40, 44, 48

Skip Count back by 4s.
48, 44, 40, 36, 32, 28, 24, 20, 16, 12, 8, 4

76 Multiplication Skill Builders   Building Math Fluency • EMC 3036 • © Evan-Moor Corp.

Page 77

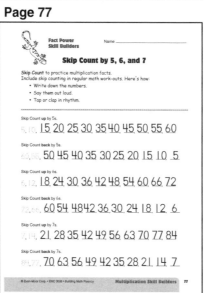

Fact Power Skill Builders

Skip Count by 5, 6, and 7

Skip Count to practice multiplication facts.
Include skip counting in regular math work-outs. Here's how:
• Write down the numbers.
• Say them out loud.
• Tap or clap in rhythm.

Skip Count up by 5s.
5, 10, 15, 20, 25, 30, 35, 40, 45, 50, 55, 60

Skip Count back by 5s.
60, 55, 50, 45, 40, 35, 30, 25, 20, 15, 10, 5

Skip Count up by 6s.
6, 12, 18, 24, 30, 36, 42, 48, 54, 60, 66, 72

Skip Count back by 6s.
72, 66, 60, 54, 48, 42, 36, 30, 24, 18, 12, 6

Skip Count up by 7s.
7, 14, 21, 28, 35, 42, 49, 56, 63, 70, 77, 84

Skip Count back by 7s.
84, 77, 70, 63, 56, 49, 42, 35, 28, 21, 14, 7

77 Multiplication Skill Builders   Building Math Fluency • EMC 3036 • © Evan-Moor Corp.

Page 78

Fact Power Skill Builders

Skip Count by 8, 9, and 12

Skip Count to practice multiplication facts.
Include skip counting in regular math work-outs. Here's how:
• Write down the numbers.
• Say them out loud.
• Tap or clap in rhythm.

Skip Count up by 8s.
8, 16, 24, 32, 40, 48, 56, 64, 72, 80, 88, 96

Skip Count back by 8s.
96, 88, 80, 72, 64, 56, 48, 40, 32, 24, 16, 8

Skip Count up by 9s.
9, 18, 27, 36, 45, 54, 63, 72, 81, 90, 99, 108

Skip Count back by 9s.
108, 99, 90, 81, 72, 63, 54, 45, 36, 27, 18, 9

Skip Count up by 12s.
12, 24, 36, 48, 60, 72, 84, 96, 108, 120, 132, 144

Skip Count back by 12s.
144, 132, 120, 108, 96, 84, 72, 60, 48, 36, 24, 12

78 Multiplication Skill Builders   Building Math Fluency • EMC 3036 • © Evan-Moor Corp.

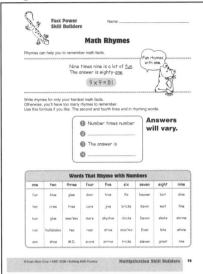

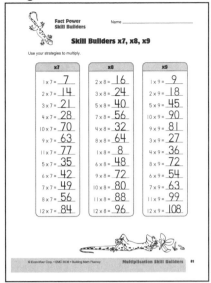

Page 79 — Math Rhymes

Rhymes can help you to remember math facts.

Nine times nine is a lot of _fun_.
The answer is eighty-_one_.

$9 \times 9 = 81$

Write rhymes for only your hardest math facts.
Otherwise, you'll have too many rhymes to remember.
Use this formula if you like. The second and fourth lines end in rhyming words.

1. Number times number
2.
3. The answer is
4.

Answers will vary.

Words That Rhyme with Numbers

one	two	three	four	five	six	seven	eight	nine
fun	blue	glee	door	hive	fix	heaven	bait	dine
ten	crew	free	core	jive	bricks	Kevin	wait	fine
bun	glue	sea/sea	more	skydive	chicks	Devon	skate	shrine
run	hullabaloo	tea	roar	drive	mix/nix	Evan	late	whine
son	shoe	M.D.	score	arrive	tricks	eleven	great	line

Page 80 — Skill Builders x4, x5, x6

Use your strategies to multiply.

x4	x5	x6
1×4 = 4	10×5 = 50	2×6 = 12
2×4 = 8	3×5 = 15	4×6 = 24
4×4 = 16	5×5 = 25	5×6 = 30
5×4 = 20	2×5 = 10	3×6 = 18
8×4 = 32	4×5 = 20	6×6 = 36
7×4 = 28	6×5 = 30	7×6 = 42
10×4 = 40	7×5 = 35	8×6 = 48
3×4 = 12	9×5 = 45	9×6 = 54
6×4 = 24	8×5 = 40	10×6 = 60
9×4 = 36	11×5 = 55	11×6 = 66
11×4 = 44	12×5 = 60	12×6 = 72
	1×5 = 5	1×6 = 6

Page 81 — Skill Builders x7, x8, x9

Use your strategies to multiply.

x7	x8	x9
1×7 = 7	2×8 = 16	1×9 = 9
2×7 = 14	3×8 = 24	2×9 = 18
3×7 = 21	5×8 = 40	5×9 = 45
4×7 = 28	7×8 = 56	10×9 = 90
10×7 = 70	4×8 = 32	9×9 = 81
9×7 = 63	8×8 = 64	3×9 = 27
11×7 = 77	1×8 = 8	4×9 = 36
5×7 = 35	6×8 = 48	8×9 = 72
6×7 = 42	9×8 = 72	6×9 = 54
7×7 = 49	10×8 = 80	7×9 = 63
8×7 = 56	11×8 = 88	11×9 = 99
12×7 = 84	12×8 = 96	12×9 = 108

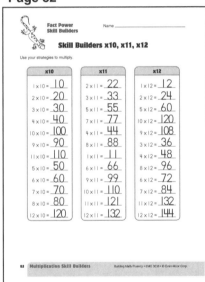

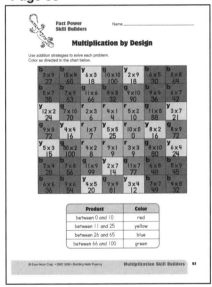

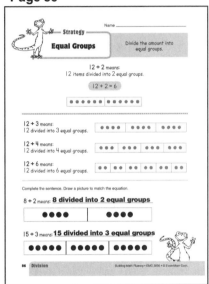

Page 82 — Skill Builders x10, x11, x12

Use your strategies to multiply.

x10	x11	x12
1×10 = 10	2×11 = 22	1×12 = 12
2×10 = 20	3×11 = 33	2×12 = 24
3×10 = 30	5×11 = 55	5×12 = 60
4×10 = 40	7×11 = 77	10×12 = 120
10×10 = 100	4×11 = 44	9×12 = 108
9×10 = 90	8×11 = 88	3×12 = 36
11×10 = 110	1×11 = 11	4×12 = 48
5×10 = 50	6×11 = 66	8×12 = 96
6×10 = 60	9×11 = 99	6×12 = 72
7×10 = 70	10×11 = 110	7×12 = 84
8×10 = 80	11×11 = 121	11×12 = 132
12×10 = 120	12×11 = 132	12×12 = 144

Page 83 — Multiplication by Design

Use addition strategies to solve each problem.
Color as directed in the chart below.

Product	Color
between 0 and 10	red
between 11 and 25	yellow
between 26 and 65	blue
between 66 and 100	green

Page 86 — Equal Groups

Divide the amount into equal groups.

$12 \div 2$ means:
12 items divided into 2 equal groups

$12 \div 2 = 6$

$12 \div 3$ means: 12 divided into 3 equal groups.

$12 \div 4$ means: 12 divided into 4 equal groups.

$12 \div 6$ means: 12 divided into 6 equal groups.

Complete the sentence. Draw a picture to match the equation.

$8 \div 2$ means: **8 divided into 2 equal groups**

$15 \div 3$ means: **15 divided into 3 equal groups**

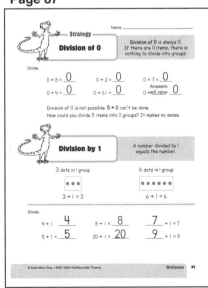

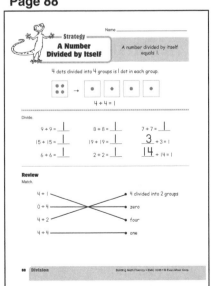

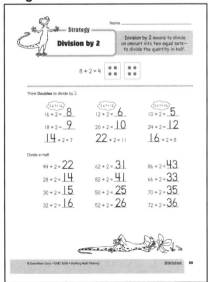

Page 87 — Division of 0

Division of 0 is always 0. If there are 0 items, there is nothing to divide into groups.

Divide.

$0 \div 8 = 0$ $0 \div 2 = 0$ $0 \div 7 = 0$
$0 \div 4 = 0$ $0 \div 61 = 0$ $0 \div 1 = 0$ **Answers will vary.**

Division of 0 is not possible. $5 \div 0$ can't be done.
How could you divide 5 items into 0 groups? It makes no sense.

Division by 1 — A number divided by 1 equals the number.

3 dots in 1 group $3 \div 1 = 3$

6 dots in 1 group $6 \div 1 = 6$

Divide.

$4 \div 1 = 4$ $8 \div 1 = 8$ $7 \div 1 = 7$
$5 \div 1 = 5$ $20 \div 1 = 20$ $9 \div 1 = 9$

Page 88 — A Number Divided by Itself

A number divided by itself equals 1.

4 dots divided into 4 groups is 1 dot in each group.

$4 \div 4 = 1$

Divide.

$9 \div 9 = 1$ $8 \div 8 = 1$ $7 \div 7 = 1$
$15 \div 15 = 1$ $19 \div 19 = 1$ $3 \div 3 = 1$
$6 \div 6 = 1$ $2 \div 2 = 1$ $14 \div 14 = 1$

Review
Match.

$4 \div 1$ — 4 divided into 2 groups
$0 \div 4$ — zero
$4 \div 2$ — four
$4 \div 4$ — one

Page 89 — Division by 2

Division by 2 means to divide an amount into two equal sets—to divide the quantity in half.

$8 \div 2 = 4$

Think **Doubles** to divide by 2.

$16 \div 2 = 8$ $12 \div 2 = 6$ $10 \div 2 = 5$
$18 \div 2 = 9$ $20 \div 2 = 10$ $24 \div 2 = 12$
$14 \div 2 = 7$ $22 \div 2 = 11$ $16 \div 2 = 8$

Divide in half.

$44 \div 2 = 22$ $62 \div 2 = 31$ $86 \div 2 = 43$
$28 \div 2 = 14$ $82 \div 2 = 41$ $66 \div 2 = 33$
$30 \div 2 = 15$ $50 \div 2 = 25$ $70 \div 2 = 35$
$32 \div 2 = 16$ $52 \div 2 = 26$ $72 \div 2 = 36$

Page 90

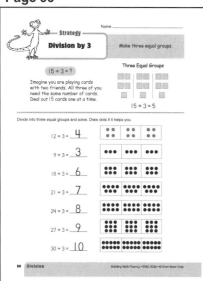

Strategy
Division by 3 — Make three equal groups.

$15 \div 3 = ?$

Imagine you are playing cards with two friends. All three of you need the same number of cards. Deal out 15 cards one at a time.

Three Equal Groups

$15 \div 3 = 5$

Divide into three equal groups and solve. Draw dots if it helps you.

$12 \div 3 = 4$
$9 \div 3 = 3$
$18 \div 3 = 6$
$21 \div 3 = 7$
$24 \div 3 = 8$
$27 \div 3 = 9$
$30 \div 3 = 10$

Page 91

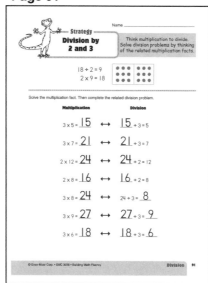

Strategy
Division by 2 and 3 — Think multiplication to divide. Solve division problems by thinking of the related multiplication facts.

$18 \div 2 = 9$
$2 \times 9 = 18$

Solve the multiplication fact. Then complete the related division problem.

Multiplication		Division
$3 \times 5 = 15$	↔	$15 \div 3 = 5$
$3 \times 7 = 21$	↔	$21 \div 3 = 7$
$2 \times 12 = 24$	↔	$24 \div 2 = 12$
$2 \times 8 = 16$	↔	$16 \div 2 = 8$
$3 \times 8 = 24$	↔	$24 \div 3 = 8$
$3 \times 9 = 27$	↔	$27 \div 3 = 9$
$3 \times 6 = 18$	↔	$18 \div 3 = 6$

Page 92

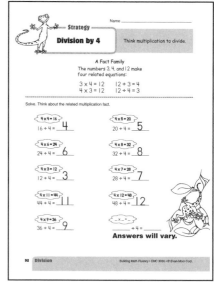

Strategy
Division by 4 — Think multiplication to divide.

A Fact Family
The numbers 3, 4, and 12 make four related equations:
$3 \times 4 = 12$ $12 \div 3 = 4$
$4 \times 3 = 12$ $12 \div 4 = 3$

Solve. Think about the related multiplication fact.

$4 \times 4 = 16$ $16 \div 4 = 4$
$4 \times 5 = 20$ $20 \div 4 = 5$
$4 \times 6 = 24$ $24 \div 4 = 6$
$4 \times 8 = 32$ $32 \div 4 = 8$
$4 \times 3 = 12$ $12 \div 4 = 3$
$4 \times 7 = 28$ $28 \div 4 = 7$
$4 \times 11 = 44$ $44 \div 4 = 11$
$4 \times 12 = 48$ $48 \div 4 = 12$
$4 \times 9 = 36$ $36 \div 4 = 9$
$\_ \times \_ = \_$ $\_ \div 4 = \_$

Answers will vary.

Page 93

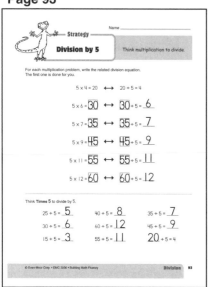

Strategy
Division by 5 — Think multiplication to divide.

For each multiplication problem, write the related division equation. The first one is done for you.

$5 \times 4 = 20$ ↔ $20 \div 5 = 4$
$5 \times 6 = 30$ ↔ $30 \div 5 = 6$
$5 \times 7 = 35$ ↔ $35 \div 5 = 7$
$5 \times 9 = 45$ ↔ $45 \div 5 = 9$
$5 \times 11 = 55$ ↔ $55 \div 5 = 11$
$5 \times 12 = 60$ ↔ $60 \div 5 = 12$

Think **Times 5** to divide by 5.

$25 \div 5 = 5$ $40 \div 5 = 8$ $35 \div 5 = 7$
$30 \div 5 = 6$ $60 \div 5 = 12$ $45 \div 5 = 9$
$15 \div 5 = 3$ $55 \div 5 = 11$ $20 \div 5 = 4$

Page 94

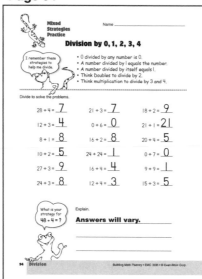

Mixed Strategies Practice
Division by 0, 1, 2, 3, 4

I remember these strategies to help me divide.

- 0 divided by any number is 0.
- A number divided by 1 equals the number.
- A number divided by itself equals 1.
- Think Doubles to divide by 2.
- Think multiplication to divide by 3 and 4.

Divide to solve the problems.

$28 \div 4 = 7$ $21 \div 3 = 7$ $18 \div 2 = 9$
$12 \div 3 = 4$ $0 \div 6 = 0$ $21 \div 1 = 21$
$8 \div 1 = 8$ $16 \div 2 = 8$ $20 \div 4 = 5$
$10 \div 2 = 5$ $24 \div 24 = 1$ $0 \div 7 = 0$
$27 \div 3 = 9$ $16 \div 4 = 4$ $9 \div 9 = 1$
$24 \div 3 = 8$ $12 \div 4 = 3$ $15 \div 3 = 5$

What is your strategy for $48 \div 4 = ?$

Explain.
Answers will vary.

Page 95

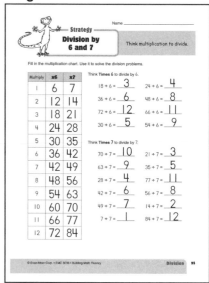

Strategy
Division by 6 and 7 — Think multiplication to divide.

Fill in the multiplication chart. Use it to solve the division problems.

Multiply	x6	x7
1	6	7
2	12	14
3	18	21
4	24	28
5	30	35
6	36	42
7	42	49
8	48	56
9	54	63
10	60	70
11	66	77
12	72	84

Think **Times 6** to divide by 6.

$18 \div 6 = 3$ $24 \div 6 = 4$
$36 \div 6 = 6$ $48 \div 6 = 8$
$72 \div 6 = 12$ $66 \div 6 = 11$
$30 \div 6 = 5$ $54 \div 6 = 9$

Think **Times 7** to divide by 7.

$70 \div 7 = 10$ $21 \div 7 = 3$
$63 \div 7 = 9$ $35 \div 7 = 5$
$28 \div 7 = 4$ $77 \div 7 = 11$
$42 \div 7 = 6$ $56 \div 7 = 8$
$49 \div 7 = 7$ $14 \div 7 = 2$
$7 \div 7 = 1$ $84 \div 7 = 12$

Page 96

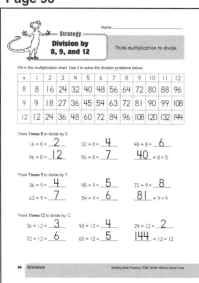

Strategy
Division by 8, 9, and 12 — Think multiplication to divide.

Fill in the multiplication chart. Use it to solve the division problems below.

x	1	2	3	4	5	6	7	8	9	10	11	12
8	8	16	24	32	40	48	56	64	72	80	88	96
9	9	18	27	36	45	54	63	72	81	90	99	108
12	12	24	36	48	60	72	84	96	108	120	132	144

Think **Times 8** to divide by 8.

$16 \div 8 = 2$ $32 \div 8 = 4$ $48 \div 8 = 6$
$96 \div 8 = 12$ $56 \div 8 = 7$ $40 \div 8 = 5$

Think **Times 9** to divide by 9.

$36 \div 9 = 4$ $45 \div 9 = 5$ $72 \div 9 = 8$
$63 \div 9 = 7$ $54 \div 9 = 6$ $81 \div 9 = 9$

Think **Times 12** to divide by 12.

$36 \div 12 = 3$ $48 \div 12 = 4$ $24 \div 12 = 2$
$72 \div 12 = 6$ $60 \div 12 = 5$ $144 \div 12 = 12$

Page 97

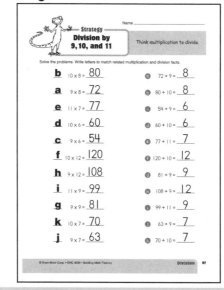

Strategy
Division by 9, 10, and 11 — Think multiplication to divide.

Solve the problems. Write letters to match related multiplication and division facts.

b $10 \times 8 = 80$ $72 \div 9 = 8$
a $9 \times 8 = 72$ $80 \div 10 = 8$
e $11 \times 7 = 77$ $54 \div 9 = 6$
d $10 \times 6 = 60$ $60 \div 10 = 6$
c $9 \times 6 = 54$ $77 \div 11 = 7$
f $10 \times 12 = 120$ $120 \div 10 = 12$
h $9 \times 12 = 108$ $81 \div 9 = 9$
i $11 \times 9 = 99$ $108 \div 9 = 12$
g $9 \times 9 = 81$ $99 \div 11 = 9$
k $10 \times 7 = 70$ $63 \div 9 = 7$
j $9 \times 7 = 63$ $70 \div 10 = 7$

Page 98

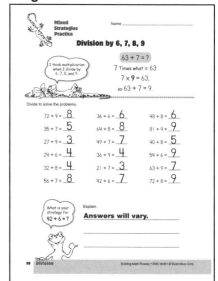

Mixed Strategies Practice
Division by 6, 7, 8, 9

$63 \div 7 = ?$

I think multiplication when I divide by 6, 7, 8, and 9.
7 Times what = 63
$7 \times 9 = 63$,
so $63 \div 7 = 9$.

Divide to solve the problems.

$72 \div 9 = 8$ $36 \div 6 = 6$ $48 \div 8 = 6$
$35 \div 7 = 5$ $64 \div 8 = 8$ $81 \div 9 = 9$
$27 \div 9 = 3$ $49 \div 7 = 7$ $40 \div 8 = 5$
$24 \div 6 = 4$ $36 \div 9 = 4$ $54 \div 6 = 9$
$32 \div 8 = 4$ $21 \div 3 = 7$ $63 \div 9 = 7$
$56 \div 7 = 8$ $42 \div 6 = 7$ $72 \div 8 = 9$

What is your strategy for $42 \div 6 = ?$

Explain.
Answers will vary.

Page 99

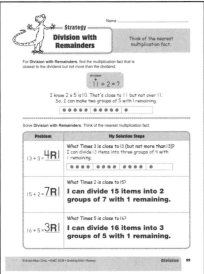

Page 100

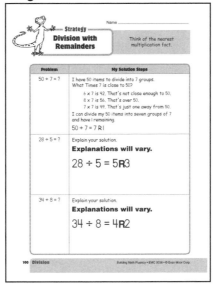

Page 101

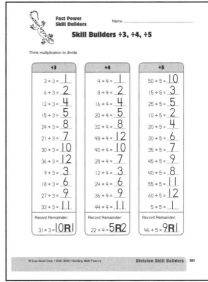

Page 102

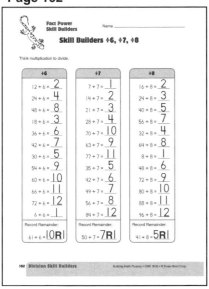

Page 103

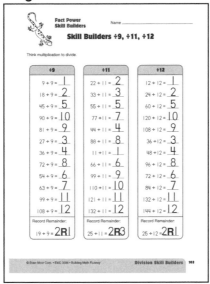

Page 104

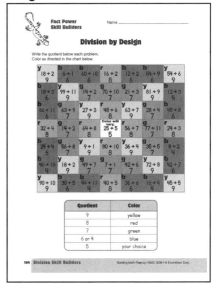

Page 106

Page 107

Page 108

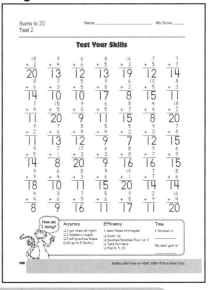

Page 109

Page 110

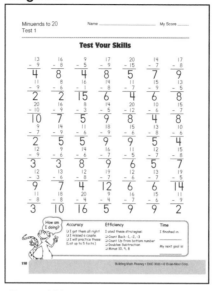

Page 111

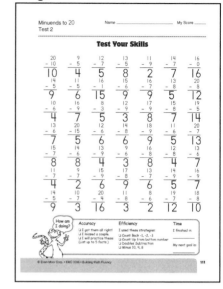

Page 112

Page 113

Page 114

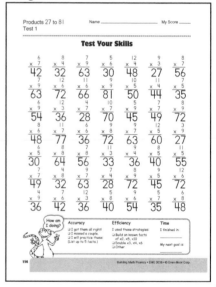

Page 115

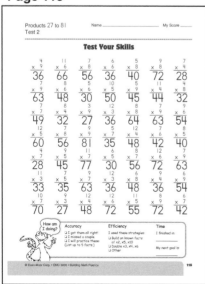

Page 116

Page 117

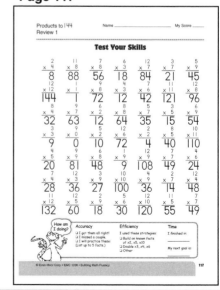

Page 118 — Products to 144, Review 2

Name _____ My Score _____

Test Your Skills

(Multiplication grid — answers shown:)
6, 16, 9, 4, 24, 36, 16
30, 64, 12, 96, 10, 48, 56
63, 8, 11, 35, 27, 90, 20
120, 60, 8, 121, 48, 81, 24
14, 72, 15, 108, 6, 45, 48
12, 132, 24, 32, 84, 21, 18
28, 40, 49, 18, 42, 25, 54

How am I doing?
Accuracy — ❏ I got them all right! ❏ I missed a couple. ❏ I will practice these: (List up to 5 facts.)
Efficiency — I used these strategies: ❏ Build on known facts of ×2, ×5, ×10 ❏ Double ×3, ×4, ×6 ❏ Other:
Time — I finished in: ___ My next goal is: ___

118   Building Math Fluency • EMC 3036 • © Evan-Moor Corp.

Page 119 — Dividends to 25, Test 1

Name _____ My Score _____

Test Your Skills

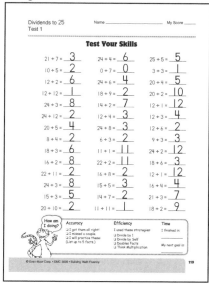

21 ÷ 7 = 3	24 ÷ 4 = 6	25 ÷ 5 = 5
10 ÷ 5 = 2	0 ÷ 7 = 0	3 ÷ 3 = 1
12 ÷ 2 = 6	24 ÷ 6 = 4	20 ÷ 2 = 10
12 ÷ 12 = 1	18 ÷ 9 = 2	20 ÷ 2 = 10
24 ÷ 3 = 8	14 ÷ 2 = 7	12 ÷ 1 = 12
24 ÷ 12 = 2	12 ÷ 4 = 3	12 ÷ 3 = 4
20 ÷ 5 = 4	24 ÷ 8 = 3	12 ÷ 6 = 2
8 ÷ 4 = 2	6 ÷ 3 = 2	9 ÷ 3 = 3
18 ÷ 3 = 6	11 ÷ 1 = 11	24 ÷ 2 = 12
16 ÷ 2 = 8	22 ÷ 2 = 11	18 ÷ 6 = 3
22 ÷ 11 = 2	16 ÷ 8 = 2	12 ÷ 1 = 12
24 ÷ 3 = 8	15 ÷ 5 = 3	16 ÷ 4 = 4
15 ÷ 3 = 5	14 ÷ 7 = 2	21 ÷ 3 = 7
20 ÷ 10 = 2	11 ÷ 11 = 1	18 ÷ 2 = 9

How am I doing?
Accuracy — ❏ I got them all right! ❏ I missed a couple. ❏ I will practice these: (List up to 5 facts.)
Efficiency — I used these strategies: ❏ Divide by 1 ❏ Divide by Self ❏ Doubles Facts ❏ Think Multiplication
Time — I finished in: ___ My next goal is: ___

© Evan-Moor Corp. • EMC 3036 • Building Math Fluency   119

Page 120 — Dividends to 25, Test 2

Name _____ My Score _____

Test Your Skills

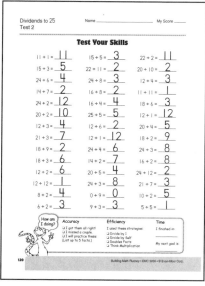

11 ÷ 1 = 11	15 ÷ 5 = 3	22 ÷ 2 = 11
15 ÷ 3 = 5	22 ÷ 11 = 2	20 ÷ 10 = 2
24 ÷ 6 = 4	24 ÷ 8 = 3	11 ÷ 11 = 1
24 ÷ 2 = 12	16 ÷ 8 = 2	18 ÷ 6 = 3
20 ÷ 2 = 10	16 ÷ 4 = 4	12 ÷ 1 = 12
12 ÷ 3 = 4	25 ÷ 5 = 5	20 ÷ 4 = 5
21 ÷ 3 = 7	12 ÷ 6 = 2	18 ÷ 2 = 9
18 ÷ 3 = 6	12 ÷ 1 = 12	24 ÷ 3 = 8
18 ÷ 2 = 9	24 ÷ 4 = 6	16 ÷ 2 = 8
12 ÷ 2 = 6	14 ÷ 2 = 7	24 ÷ 12 = 2
12 ÷ 12 = 1	20 ÷ 5 = 4	21 ÷ 7 = 3
8 ÷ 2 = 4	24 ÷ 3 = 8	10 ÷ 2 = 5
	0 ÷ 9 = 0	5 ÷ 5 = 1

How am I doing?
Accuracy — ❏ I got them all right! ❏ I missed a couple. ❏ I will practice these: (List up to 5 facts.)
Efficiency — I used these strategies: ❏ Divide by 1 ❏ Divide by Self ❏ Doubles Facts ❏ Think Multiplication
Time — I finished in: ___ My next goal is: ___

120   Building Math Fluency • EMC 3036 • © Evan-Moor Corp.

Page 121 — Dividends 27 to 81, Test 1

Name _____ My Score _____

Test Your Skills

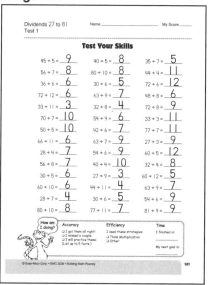

45 ÷ 5 = 9	40 ÷ 5 = 8	35 ÷ 7 = 5
56 ÷ 7 = 8	80 ÷ 10 = 8	44 ÷ 4 = 11
36 ÷ 6 = 6	30 ÷ 6 = 5	72 ÷ 6 = 12
72 ÷ 12 = 6	63 ÷ 9 = 7	48 ÷ 8 = 6
33 ÷ 11 = 3	32 ÷ 8 = 4	72 ÷ 9 = 8
70 ÷ 7 = 10	54 ÷ 9 = 6	33 ÷ 3 = 11
50 ÷ 5 = 10	42 ÷ 6 = 7	77 ÷ 7 = 11
66 ÷ 11 = 6	63 ÷ 7 = 9	27 ÷ 3 = 9
28 ÷ 4 = 7	54 ÷ 6 = 9	60 ÷ 5 = 12
56 ÷ 8 = 7	40 ÷ 4 = 10	32 ÷ 4 = 8
30 ÷ 5 = 6	27 ÷ 9 = 3	60 ÷ 12 = 5
60 ÷ 10 = 6	44 ÷ 11 = 4	63 ÷ 9 = 7
28 ÷ 7 = 4	30 ÷ 6 = 5	54 ÷ 6 = 9
80 ÷ 10 = 8	77 ÷ 11 = 7	81 ÷ 9 = 9

How am I doing?
Accuracy — ❏ I got them all right! ❏ I missed a couple. ❏ I will practice these: (List up to 5 facts.)
Efficiency — I used these strategies: ❏ Think Multiplication ❏ Other:
Time — I finished in: ___ My next goal is: ___

© Evan-Moor Corp. • EMC 3036 • Building Math Fluency   121

Page 122 — Dividends 27 to 81, Test 2

Name _____ My Score _____

Test Your Skills

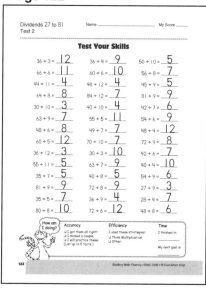

36 ÷ 3 = 12	36 ÷ 4 = 9	50 ÷ 10 = 5
66 ÷ 6 = 11	60 ÷ 6 = 10	56 ÷ 8 = 7
44 ÷ 11 = 4	48 ÷ 12 = 4	45 ÷ 9 = 5
64 ÷ 8 = 8	84 ÷ 12 = 7	81 ÷ 9 = 9
30 ÷ 10 = 3	40 ÷ 10 = 4	42 ÷ 7 = 6
63 ÷ 9 = 7	55 ÷ 5 = 11	54 ÷ 6 = 9
48 ÷ 6 = 8	49 ÷ 7 = 7	48 ÷ 4 = 12
60 ÷ 5 = 12	70 ÷ 10 = 7	72 ÷ 9 = 8
36 ÷ 12 = 3	30 ÷ 3 = 10	42 ÷ 6 = 7
55 ÷ 11 = 5	63 ÷ 7 = 9	40 ÷ 4 = 10
35 ÷ 7 = 5	72 ÷ 8 = 9	54 ÷ 9 = 6
81 ÷ 9 = 9	36 ÷ 9 = 4	27 ÷ 9 = 3
35 ÷ 5 = 7	36 ÷ 9 = 4	28 ÷ 4 = 7
80 ÷ 8 = 10	72 ÷ 6 = 12	48 ÷ 8 = 6

How am I doing?
Accuracy — ❏ I got them all right! ❏ I missed a couple. ❏ I will practice these: (List up to 5 facts.)
Efficiency — I used these strategies: ❏ Think Multiplication ❏ Other:
Time — I finished in: ___ My next goal is: ___

122   Building Math Fluency • EMC 3036 • © Evan-Moor Corp.

Page 123 — Dividends 84 to 144

Name _____ My Score _____

Test Your Skills

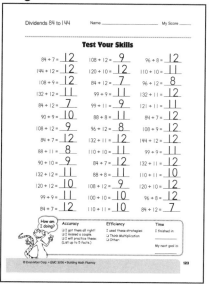

84 ÷ 7 = 12	108 ÷ 12 = 9	96 ÷ 8 = 12
144 ÷ 12 = 12	120 ÷ 10 = 12	110 ÷ 10 = 11
108 ÷ 9 = 12	84 ÷ 12 = 7	96 ÷ 12 = 8
132 ÷ 12 = 11	99 ÷ 9 = 11	132 ÷ 11 = 12
84 ÷ 12 = 7	99 ÷ 11 = 9	121 ÷ 11 = 11
90 ÷ 10 = 9	88 ÷ 8 = 11	84 ÷ 7 = 12
108 ÷ 9 = 12	96 ÷ 12 = 8	108 ÷ 9 = 12
84 ÷ 7 = 12	132 ÷ 11 = 12	144 ÷ 12 = 12
88 ÷ 11 = 8	110 ÷ 10 = 11	99 ÷ 9 = 11
90 ÷ 10 = 9	84 ÷ 7 = 12	132 ÷ 11 = 12
132 ÷ 12 = 11	88 ÷ 8 = 11	110 ÷ 11 = 10
120 ÷ 12 = 10	108 ÷ 12 = 9	96 ÷ 8 = 12
99 ÷ 9 = 11	100 ÷ 10 = 10	96 ÷ 8 = 12
84 ÷ 7 = 12	110 ÷ 11 = 10	84 ÷ 12 = 7

How am I doing?
Accuracy — ❏ I got them all right! ❏ I missed a couple. ❏ I will practice these: (List up to 5 facts.)
Efficiency — I used these strategies: ❏ Think Multiplication ❏ Other:
Time — I finished in: ___ My next goal is: ___

© Evan-Moor Corp. • EMC 3036 • Building Math Fluency   123

Page 124 — Dividends to 144, Review 1

Name _____ My Score _____

Test Your Skills

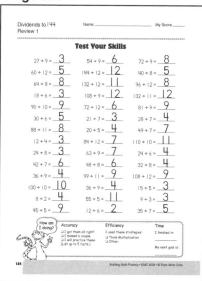

27 ÷ 9 = 3	54 ÷ 9 = 6	72 ÷ 9 = 8
60 ÷ 12 = 5	144 ÷ 12 = 12	40 ÷ 8 = 5
64 ÷ 8 = 8	132 ÷ 12 = 11	96 ÷ 12 = 8
18 ÷ 6 = 3	108 ÷ 9 = 12	132 ÷ 11 = 12
90 ÷ 10 = 9	72 ÷ 12 = 6	81 ÷ 9 = 9
30 ÷ 6 = 5	21 ÷ 7 = 3	28 ÷ 7 = 4
88 ÷ 11 = 8	20 ÷ 5 = 4	49 ÷ 7 = 7
12 ÷ 4 = 3	84 ÷ 12 = 7	110 ÷ 10 = 11
24 ÷ 8 = 3	63 ÷ 9 = 7	24 ÷ 6 = 4
42 ÷ 7 = 6	48 ÷ 8 = 6	32 ÷ 8 = 4
36 ÷ 9 = 4	99 ÷ 11 = 9	108 ÷ 12 = 9
100 ÷ 10 = 10	36 ÷ 9 = 4	15 ÷ 5 = 3
8 ÷ 2 = 4	55 ÷ 5 = 11	9 ÷ 3 = 3
45 ÷ 9 = 5	12 ÷ 6 = 2	35 ÷ 7 = 5

How am I doing?
Accuracy — ❏ I got them all right! ❏ I missed a couple. ❏ I will practice these: (List up to 5 facts.)
Efficiency — I used these strategies: ❏ Think Multiplication ❏ Other:
Time — I finished in: ___ My next goal is: ___

124   Building Math Fluency • EMC 3036 • © Evan-Moor Corp.

Page 125 — Dividends to 144, Review 2

Name _____ My Score _____

Test Your Skills

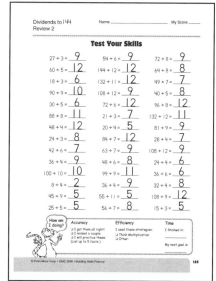

27 ÷ 3 = 9	54 ÷ 6 = 9	72 ÷ 8 = 9
60 ÷ 5 = 12	144 ÷ 12 = 12	64 ÷ 8 = 8
18 ÷ 3 = 6	132 ÷ 11 = 12	49 ÷ 7 = 7
90 ÷ 9 = 10	132 ÷ 11 = 12	40 ÷ 5 = 8
30 ÷ 5 = 6	72 ÷ 6 = 12	96 ÷ 8 = 12
88 ÷ 8 = 11	21 ÷ 3 = 7	132 ÷ 12 = 11
48 ÷ 4 = 12	20 ÷ 4 = 5	81 ÷ 9 = 9
24 ÷ 3 = 8	84 ÷ 7 = 12	28 ÷ 4 = 7
36 ÷ 4 = 9	48 ÷ 6 = 8	108 ÷ 12 = 9
100 ÷ 10 = 10	99 ÷ 9 = 11	24 ÷ 4 = 6
8 ÷ 4 = 2	36 ÷ 4 = 9	32 ÷ 4 = 8
45 ÷ 9 = 5	55 ÷ 11 = 5	108 ÷ 9 = 12
25 ÷ 5 = 5	56 ÷ 7 = 8	15 ÷ 3 = 5

How am I doing?
Accuracy — ❏ I got them all right! ❏ I missed a couple. ❏ I will practice these: (List up to 5 facts.)
Efficiency — I used these strategies: ❏ Think Multiplication ❏ Other:
Time — I finished in: ___ My next goal is: ___

© Evan-Moor Corp. • EMC 3036 • Building Math Fluency   125

Multiplication Table

x	1	2	3	4	5	6	7	8	9	10
1										
2										
3										
4										
5										
6										
7										
8										
9										
10										